Samkhya Karika

"The Samkhya Karika conveys the core ideas underlying the practice of yoga. The witness or seer (purusha) can only find freedom by understanding and purifying his relationship to the manifest world of the body and senses (prakriti). In this elegant new translation, Srivatsa Ramaswami provides easy access to this important text. Explanatory cross-references connect the Samkhya to Patañjali's Yoga Sutra and Krishna's wisdom in the Bhagavad Gita. All serious students of yoga will benefit from reading and learning the 25 principles of Samkhya as described in these 72 verses."

Christopher Key Chapple, Doshi professor of Indic and Comparative Theology and founding director of the Master of Arts in Yoga Studies at Loyola Marymount University

"The Samkhya Karika is the core text of Samkhya, and Samkhya is the master key to unlocking the secrets of both Patañjali's yoga Sutras and Vedanta. Srivatsa Ramaswami, one of the few remaining living disciples of T. Krishnamacharya, has translated the text, including word-for-word breakdowns, and provided his personal commentary based on extensive study and practice. Ramaswami is a man of great integrity, and this is a wonderful resource for all serious students of yoga. Highly recommended!"

Ranju Roy, author of *Yoga as Pilgrimage* and coauthor of *Embodying the Yoga Sutras*

"Srivatsa Ramaswami's translation of the Samkhya Karika is a boon to every yoga student, teacher, and spiritual seeker. This book and its tools illuminate the way to freedom from suffering and understanding of the Self. It is a rare gem that provides access to the teachings of yoga beyond asana. This book is more than a superb technical exposition and an engaging read. Srivatsa Ramaswami's lifelong dedication to study and practice shines throughout this text. His sincerity, honesty, wisdom, wit, clarity, and expertise help the reader better understand the path of yoga and the nature of the Self. If you are looking to immerse yourself in yoga, look no further than this book. It is truly a gift for anyone on the path to truth."

Ryan Leier, founder of One Yoga and Vinyasa Yoga for Youth and a student of the Krishnamacharya yoga lineage

"The Samkhya Karika is an essential scripture for understanding yogic thought and instrumental in building the fundamental teachings of Sanātana Dharma. With several decades of experience teaching yoga and Vedanta, no one is more qualified to translate the Samkhya Karika than Srivatsa Ramaswami. This version is destined to become the traditional authority on this important ancient text in the pantheon of Dharmic philosophy."

Jason Gregory, author of *The Science and Practice of Humility*, *Enlightenment Now*, and *Effortless Living*

"This book is a true treasure trove for those seeking a deeper understanding of Samkhya philosophy presented in a simple conversational style. Generously sprinkled with stories and anecdotes shared with subtle humor, it is bound to keep you engaged. The explanations are supported by interesting references drawn from a huge repository of knowledge that testifies to the author's mastery of yoga, Samkhya, and all related subjects. For those of us from this tradition who have not met Sri Krishnamacharya, Srivatsa Ramaswami's simple presence and generous sharing helps us get a glimpse of the great master and the depth of his mastery. For students of yoga, this book will remain an important reference and inspiration to deepen our self-inquiry and understanding of the mysteries of life, touching the many subtle layers of our existence and leading us on the path to light and truth!"

Saraswathi Vasudevan, founder and director of YogaVahini and student of Sri TKV Desikachar

Samkhya Karika

A YOGA PRACTITIONER'S GUIDE TO OVERCOMING THE THREE CAUSES OF SUFFERING

सांख्यकारिका

Srivatsa Ramaswami

Inner Traditions
Rochester, Vermont

Inner Traditions
One Park Street
Rochester, Vermont 05767
www.InnerTraditions.com

Cataloging-in-Publication Data for this title is available from the Library of Congress

ISBN 979-8-88850-153-5 (print)
ISBN 979-8-88850-154-2 (ebook)

Printed and bound in China by Reliance Printing Co., Ltd.

10 9 8 7 6 5 4 3 2 1

Text design and layout by Virginia Scott Bowman
This book was typeset in Garamond Premier Pro and Gill Sans with Ancient Zurich used as the display typeface

To send correspondence to the author of this book, mail a first-class letter to the author c/o Inner Traditions • Bear & Company, One Park Street, Rochester, VT 05767, and we will forward the communication.

CONTENTS

SLOKAS OF THE SAMKHYA KARIKA BY TOPIC

A NOTE ON THE TRANSLATION

This book necessarily contains many Sanskrit terms, which we have rendered into more user-friendly English in the text. I encourage serious students of Samkhya, Yoga, and Vedanta to try to get some basic knowledge of the ancient root language of Sanskrit. In times past, anyone whose mother tongue was English or some other language had great difficulty learning Sanskrit, especially as it is rendered in nagari characters. But now with the advent of various Sanskrit translation sites on the internet, it is much easier to acquire a working knowledge of basic Sanskrit. If someone takes the trouble to learn and thoroughly understand a minimum vocabulary of say about three hundred Sanskrit terms and words predominantly found in Vedic philosophical works, they would find it to be immensely helpful. A glossary is also provided beginning on page 198 of this book.

PREFACE

My Vedic initiation (*upanayana*) took place when I was about ten years old. I used to wake up around six in the morning and do my morning *sandhya*, a sun worship ritual in which I did 108 Gayatri mantra recitations, or *japa*, and ten rounds of *samantraka pranayama*, the practice of pranayama accompanied by mantra recitation that allows one to totally immerse one's mind in the mantra. One day I woke up around five a.m. and heard some muffled voices downstairs. Curious, I went down and opened the puja room door. There I found my father learning to chant Vedic mantras from a young teacher, a student at the famous Madras Sanskrit College. I quickly brushed my teeth and washed my face, then sat down next to my father and started repeating each mantra twice, along with my father. Neither the teacher nor my father raised any objection. This went on for about an hour. Afterward I learned that it was the first chapter of the Vedic text known as the Taittiriya Aranyaka, which consists of the well-known Aruna Surya Namaskara* mantras. Thereafter I continued to study along with my father

*The sun gives continuously, but never takes; *runa* means "debt," so *aruna* means "unindebted." The sun is credited with removing the burden of debt of those who worship him with the Surya Namaskara and Aruna Surya Namaskara mantras. Further, sun worship is said to take care of the three debt burdens every human being is said to carry: the debt to parents/forefathers known as *pitru runa*; those debts one owes to gods of nature like fire (*agni devata*), wind (*vayu devata*), rain (*varuna devata*), and others known as *deva runa*; and the indebtedness to sages who have given knowledge or *rishi runa*.

up until the end of the text, and then later I learned the earlier portions that I had missed. In the course of the next four years, I learned how to chant a number of Vedic Sanskrit works commonly taught in South India, such as the ancient Vedic chant known as the Rudram Chamakam, the hymns of the Vedas known as *suktas*, and the Taittiriya and Mahanarayana Upanishads from the Yajurveda, an ancient collection of mantras used in Vedic rituals. The teacher also taught some well-known Sanskrit verses, or *slokas*, such as the Vishnu Sahasranama and the Chandrasekharashtakam and Shankaracharya's Dakshiamurti Stotram. While the other slokas were accessible, the Dakshinanmurti slokas, which explain the source and metaphysics of the universe from the advaita Vedanta perspective, were not understandable. I asked my teacher to explain them, but he told me that I should learn to chant it first, then later on in life I could try to understand the philosophy behind it.

My studies with the young teacher ended after four years, when he left the city.

I first started studying with Sri Krishnamacharya in 1955, and he remained my guru until his passing in 1988. Initially and for several years it was all "on the cotton mat" yoga. It was all cotton mats at that time and not the synthetic stuff commonly used in the West and everywhere nowadays. He taught a wonderful breath-oriented yoga asana practice that included hundreds of vinyasas in scores of asana sequences that included synchronized breathing. He called his system, which I now use in my own teachings, *vinyasa krama*.* Thereafter and for several years I studied Vedic chanting with Sri Krishnamacharya, covering almost the entire Taittiriya Aranyaka. At that point he started teaching the important texts he thought a yoga

*In Sanskrit, the prefix *vi* means "variety," *nyasa* means "placement," and *krama* means "sequence" or "methodology."

student should study if so inclined. He started with the Yoga Sutras of Patanjali—every sutra, word by word. Other texts followed: the Samkhya Karika of the fourth-century sage Ishvarakrishna, with commentary by sixth-century Vedic philosopher Gaudapada and some of the classic treatises of Hatha yoga—the Hatha Yoga Pradipika, the Gherunda Samhita, Yoga Yagnyavalkya, and the Siva Samhita. But before that he taught the Bhagavad Gita, which he considered an important Yoga text just as it is considered an important Vedanta text. Thereafter he taught the Brahma Sutras and many vidyas or topics of the major Upanishads, such as the Chandogya, Brihadaranyaka, Prasna, Mundaka, Taittiriya, Mandukya, Kausitaki Brahmana, Svetaswatara, Katha, Kena, Aitareya, and a few others. In all, this course of study took three decades for me to complete.

After my guru's passing, I decided to retire from my work in finance and investment and start teaching as much of what I had absorbed from my wonderful teacher as I could. I didn't realize it at the time I was studying with him but I later came to discover that Sri Krishnamacharya was very famous, well-known all over the world, yet most of his teachings were completely unknown in the western yoga world. Even the asana practice I found was being taught in India and elsewhere in the world was much different from the vinyasa krama yoga he taught in all the years I had studied with him. His vinyasa krama system was predominately breath-oriented and based on the correct interpretation of the term *prayatna saitilya*, translated as "effortless life effort (breath)," a description of smoothing the breath in aesthetic vinyasa variations. So, I told myself that I would endeavor to teach as many of the subjects I had learned from him as I could, as I loved what he taught and how he taught. Nothing touched me as deeply and was as fulfilling as his teachings on the ancient wisdoms. I thought there may be a few yoga enthusiasts who will resonate with these teachings as deeply as I had, so sort of lonely.

Loyola Marymount University in Los Angeles gave me ample opportunities to teach, and I initially taught yoga according to Krishnamacharya's method of vinyasa krama. Then in 2000 I published my book *Yoga for the Three Stages of Life* (Inner Traditions). In it, I gave a comprehensive view of yoga as articulated by Patanjali, following the thought process behind it. It had a fair amount of discussion and teachings on asana, but it also had other aspects of yoga that in my view are not sufficiently emphasized in modern yoga books or in studios. Then in 2005 I published *The Complete Book of Vinyasa Yoga* (DaCapo Press), which I have used as a textbook in my 200- and 100-hour yoga teacher training programs, taught many times in different places.

Around this same time, I recorded many of the Vedic chants and other popular Sanskrit devotional works that I had learned from Sri Krishnamacharya, using a leading company in Madras, India, the Master Recording Company. An album, titled *Sundara Kanda*, runs close to ten hours and includes the Sundara Kanda, the fifth "beautiful chapter" in the Hindu epic the Ramayana, of more than 2800 verses. Other major chants that I recorded include a three-hour recitation of the Aswamedha ritual (described later); the Mooka Pancha Sati, a 500-sloka classic on the goddess Kanchi Kamakshi Devi; the Devi Mahatmayam, or "Glory of the Goddess"; and many of the *sahasranamas* (thousand names) mantras of popular deities such as Shiva, Vishnu, Ganesha, Lalita, Durga, Subrahmanya, Gayatri, Anjaneya, Raghavendra, and others.*

Thereafter I offered teachings to yoga practitioners on a number of Vedic treatises at Loyola Marymount and other locations around the world: the Bhagavad Gita, the Yoga Sutras

---

*Almost all of these Sanskrit chants are still available on my YouTube page, "Ramaswami Srivatsa," and also on Spotify, JioSaavan, and other platforms.

of Patanjali, the Samkhya Karika, Sri Krishnamacharya's Nathamuni Yoga Rahasya, the Yoga Yajnavalkya, the Hatayogapradipika, and the Upanishad Vidyas. Some of my talks on the Gita and the Samkhya Karika were filmed and can be found on YouTube,* as were talks on other yoga-related subjects such as "Yoga for the Internal Organs." My twenty-hour lecture series on the Samkhya Karika, which took place at Yoga Vahini, a yoga teacher training facility in Chennai, India, was transcribed by a team chosen from among the participants, and this has become the basis of the book you are reading now.† While preparing this book, I also recorded a recitation of the complete Samkhya Karika.§

I am now eighty-five years old. Although yoga is multidimensional, most modern books on yoga deal exclusively with asana practice, so my goal for my remaining years is to continue to teach and publish works on the foundational subjects of yoga that Krishnamacharya taught, and so the book you now hold in your hands, the Samkhya Karika for yoga practitioners, is the fruit of my labors.

---

*The YouTube videos were expertly edited by my friend Jacquelin Sonderling.

†I am grateful to Jyoti Shanbag, Suchitra Sohoni, Anita Balasubramaniam, Enika Planovszky, Pratibha Varadarajan, and Savitri Ravikrishnan for their hard work in transcribing the teachings from these lectures. And also, to Saraswathi Vasudevan for sponsoring so many yoga programs, including this one in Chennai, India.

§ This can be found on my YouTube channel and is titled "Samkhya Karika Recitation Srivatsa Ramaswami."

INTRODUCTION TO THE SAMKHYA KARIKA

There are six *darshanas*, or schools of philosophy, associated with the Vedas. They are the Vaiseshika, Nyaya, Mimamsa, Samkhya, Yoga, and Vedanta schools. The latter three are called *nivritti shastras,** that is, philosophies that teach us how to reach a complete state of freedom from rebirth. Samkhya in particular is a groundbreaking Vedic philosophy in this regard. This school, based on several Vedic mantras, is said to have been founded by the sixth century BCE sage Kapila, while its definitive treatise was written in the fourth century CE by the philosopher and poet Ishvarakrishna. It is said that Samkhya schools postulated the existence of the Self, or atman, as distinctly different from the body-mind complex, which is merely the physical self yet is usually mistaken for being the true Self, the atman, by most everyone in the modern world.

Both Yoga and Vedanta, the other two nivritti philosophies, totally embrace the Samkhya view of the Self as pure, unvarying consciousness and hence immortal, even though there

*The word *nivritti* is *vritti* with the prefix *ni*. *Vritti* means "activity," and *nivritti* signifies activity associated with avoiding something one does not want. What is that which is unwanted? It is future pain, especially rebirth. So, practices and systems that help us avoid future pain and especially future births would be nivritti shastras.

are some clear differences among the three nivritti philosophies. Samkhyas—those who embrace the path of Samkhya—are a proud lot. They would say that theirs is the only comprehensive philosophy that can free the mind of any doubts about the essential things one has to know: the origin of the universe, its evolution, and the nature of the subject in a subject-object relationship. Panchashikha, one of the earliest teachers of the Samkhya philosophy, said of Samkhya,

एकमेव दर्शनं साम्ख्यमेव दर्शनम्।

ekameva darśanaṃsāmkhyameva darśanam |

There is only one *darshana*, or complete exposition, and that is Samkhya philosophy.

The Samkhya Karika is hailed as a masterpiece by many Sanskrit scholars for its literary and philosophical content. Ishvarakrishna, the author, is considered an avatar of the fifth-century classical Sanskrit poet Kalidasa. Sri Krishnamacharya taught all seventy-two slokas of Ishvarakrishna's text word by word, over a long period of time.

Ishvarakrishna's Samkhya treatise is written in Arya meter,* a poetic rhythm unique to Sanskrit. In Arya meter, the sloka consists of four lines, or *padas*, meaning "feet" or "quarters." In this meter, every short syllable is taken as one time measure (*maatra*), and long syllables are treated as two time measures. In addition, a short vowel or syllable followed by two consonants is treated as two time measures, or a compound letter like

*For example, the first chapter in Mookapanchasati, a 500-verse devotional outpouring on the supreme goddess of beauty and tranquility, Kanchi Kamakshi, and some works by the poet Kalidasa, are also in Arya meter. You can find a video of me chanting the Mookapanchasati on YouTube titled "Sanskrit—Mooka Panchashathi, H. H. Shri Shri Jayendra Saraswathi Swamigal, Srivatsa Ramaswami." The first chapter is "Arya Satakam" (one hundred verses in Arya Meter).

khya in *samkhya* will be two time measures, even if it is a short syllable. This makes for a very beautiful and rhythmic pattern when chanting these slokas. Chanting the Samkhya Karika is a wonderful experience.

Samkhya philosophy provides a thorough and very logical explanation of three essential areas one should know: 1) the origin of the universe, 2) its evolution, and 3) the nature of the Self. Another of the three nivritti shastras, Yoga, takes a lot from Samkhya by developing it into a practical system, including the development of unique yogic mental discipline to achieve the Samkhya goal of liberation from cyclic existence, known as *kaivalya*.

The word *samkhya* translates as "enumeration" or sometimes as "perfect declaration." This explains the aim of Samkhya: to take into account all the important factors of the world, especially those related to the human condition, and to enumerate those basic aspects of reality so that we can understand them and thereby find liberation. There are twenty-five *tattvas*, or aspects of reality, elaborated in this doctrine. Taken together, the tattvas account for the totality of the universe as a whole, as well as the true Self in each individual human being.

What is a karika? It comes from the root *kru*, "to do," or "to work." What kind of work? Here it is a literary work, an investigative philosophical work. The suffix *ka* indicates a container or a book that contains this philosophical work. The karikas are written as verses, or slokas. The meanings are usually very dense, somewhat like the sutras. Karikas like the Samkhya Karika excel not only in their philosophical content, but also in their literary value. Ishvarakrishna is both a great philosopher and a poet. There are not many karika works. The most famous are the Samkhya Karika, which expounds on Samkhya philosophy, and the Mandukya Karika by Gaudapada, who was the guru of Adi Shankara's mentor Govinda Bhagavatpada. The Mandukya

Karika is written as an exposition of Advaita Vedanta philosophy as developed around the OM or pranava mantra found in the Mandukya Upanished. Both the Samkhya Karika and the Mandukya Karika are highly revered works of Vedic philosophy, one on Samkhya and the other on Advaita Vedanta philosophy.

This book explains the meaning of each karika, analyzing the verses word-by-word. You will find the original Sanskrit, a transliteration of the Sanskrit, an English-language translation, followed by additional commentary. In some of the karikas I've also included some of the most common questions from my students, and my replies to those questions.

Samkhya Karika

Translation and Commentary

Kārikā 1

The need to unearth the definitive means of removing suffering

दुःखत्रयाभिघाताज्जिज्ञासा तदपघातके हेतौ ।
दृष्टेसापार्थाचेन्नैकान्तात्यन्ततोऽभावात् ॥ १॥

Duḥkhatrayābhighātājjijñāsātadapaghātakehetau ।
dṛṣṭesāpārthācennaikāntātyantato'bhāvāt ||1||

duḥkha—vitiated mental space, suffering, pain
traya—three types or causes
abhighātāt—injured, intolerable
jijñāsā—desire to know, discussion
tat—refers to the three types of duhkha
apaghātake—destroy
hetau—means
dṛṣṭe—all already known
apārthā—therefore aimless, goalless
cet—if so said
na—no
ekāntāt—definite
antatah—permanent
abhāvāt—absent

// Having repeatedly been tormented by the three types or sources of suffering, or *duhkha*, there is a desire to know (*jijnasa*) the means to remove duhkha. However, if it be said that the means are already known and available, then those known, available means suffer from not being definitive

(*ekantata abhavat*) and not being permanent (*atyantata abhavat*). //

Notably, the Samkhya Karika of Ishvarakrishna starts with the word *duhkha*, "suffering." There are three causes of duhkha. The first cause is produced by afflictions of the body and mind. *Vyadhi* refers to physical illnesses like fever. Those afflictions caused by the mind like desire, anger, anxiety, depression, disappointment, and others are known as *adhi*. Pain inflicted by or caused by other beings such as insects, animals, and other human beings is called *adhibhautika*. The third cause of suffering, literally called acts of god *(adhidaivika)*, is brought about by nature. Floods, fires, earthquakes, and tornadoes come under this category. *Deva* means divine or god and *deivika* would be of god or acts of god. According to puranas (Indian mythology) all of nature is governd by different gods like Varuna for rain, Agni for fire, and so on. So *adhidaivika* would be the damage or pain cased by acts of gods or nature.

The text says that the known means of overcoming these causes of suffering are subject to impermanence and uncertainty. For instance, if one suffers from hypertension, the medication one has to take may work for some but may not work at all; moreover, it will not cure the condition permanently. Likewise, mental afflictions like desire, anger, and so forth are seldom fully eradicated. Sometimes we succeed in getting what we want, sometimes partially, and mostly not at all. The degree of success in our endeavors is less than perfect, and the mind is never satisfied. Even if one is satisfied, the satisfaction does not stay for long. So, the Samkhya Karika says one has to find a definitive and permanent solution, one has to find remedies to remove these pains permanently and perfectly. The Samkhya system does precisely that.

Here is a famous quote from Kumarila Bhatta,

प्रयोजनम् अनुद्दिश्य न मन्दोऽपि प्रवर्तते ।

prayojanam anuddiśya na mando'pi pravartate

Even a dimwit will not undertake any activity without knowing its benefits.

Without knowing the benefit of an activity, why undertake it? In the same way, why should people study Samkhya? Because the goal of Samkhya is to reach the state of liberation, or *kaivalya*, through deep contemplation. To be liberated is to be unafflicted; it is to be eternally free. But then, free from what? Free from the endless cycle of birth and death. Trapped in the cycle of samsara, life is mostly painful. Many may counter that by wondering, *Even though there is pain in life, surely there is also pleasure*. But to the discerning minds of sages like Kapila or Patanjali, life is full of duhkha, and all the efforts to eradicate it definitively and forever are futile. Shankaracharya, Kapila, Patanjali, and indeed sages throughout time have felt the suffering of human beings who do not or cannot take the necessary steps to end the painful and purposeless cycle of samsara. Most people seek pleasure and happiness in life; they rise with the tide and roll with the punches, traveling through life clueless.

It could be said that conditions during the time of Kapila or Shankaracharya were relatively primitive. Today things have changed. Science has made life so much better. Many diseases have been completely eliminated. Rapid advances in cancer treatment, heart disease, and diabetes have helped prolong lives. Overall, people are living longer and healthier than during Ishvarakrishna's time. Yet people are still unhappy. In the Yoga Vasishta, the authorship of which is attributed to sage Valmiki and which is considered a definitive text for spiritual aspirants, there is the tale of two siddha yogis. Both had the siddhi of traveling in time. They wanted to see if people would be happier in the future compared to the past. One went back in time and the other went into the future. After an elaborate study, they met to discuss their findings. The yogi who had gone back in time said that he found that most people were unhappy in the past and happy only one-sixteenth of the time. The siddha yogi who went into the future said that despite enormous material progress, people were happy only one-sixteenth of the time.

Most people work their butts off just to make ends meet. Many die without resources in old age or even in debt. And then there are the emotional issues that cannot be resolved by power, possessions, love, or attention. In fact, more people today appear to have emotional problems, whether rich, poor, or famous. Antidepressants are prescribed, but most people are not helped by these drugs. People go about their lives without knowing who they really are or what they want. So, the means generally offered for eradicating suffering are at best temporary and do not offer a permanent or a definitive cure.

Samkhyas rightfully have concerns about pain and sorrow in future lives. Many other Eastern philosophies also subscribe to the theory of karma. And this law, like any law, does not excuse ignorance or lack of faith in karmic law. Hence all these philosophical systems want us as a matter of self-interest to find a way to end the painful cycle of samsara and achieve eternal freedom from pain and sorrow. Sri Krishnamacharya, in his book *Nathamuni's Yoga Rahasya*, quotes extensively from the Vishnu Purana, an ancient text that is a complete narrative, from the creation of the current universe to its destruction. In it, Vyasa, the author, drives home the need to address the perennial sorrow that characterizes samsara and the steps to remedy it, such as by taking up appropriate activities like yoga and wisdom.

In Vishnu Purana, Parasara told Maitreyi:

"Oh! Maitreyi! The three afflictions, *adhyatmika*, *adhibhautika*, and *adhidaivika*, can be taken care of by developing *jnana* [wisdom of the Self] and *vairagya* [dispassion]. Adhyatmika is what one makes of oneself—is of two types, of body and of mind. The ailments of the body are numerous. They affect the body in many ways and ultimately destroy it. There are many ailments—headache[s] and [conditions] of the head. Then there are diseases of the lungs, fevers, stomach pain and ulcers, problems of the spleen, fistula, edema of organs, vomiting, and others. Then eye ailments, indigestion, diarrhea, and many more that afflict the body. Then there are issues of the mind: intense desire and anger, fear, greed, infatuation, sorrow, jealousy, humiliation, intolerance, fault-finding, gossiping, rumor-mongering, back-biting, and more.

The *adhibhautika* pain is caused by animals, birds, and cruel people and other creatures. And the suffering caused by heat, wind, cold, rain, and lightning and other natural causes are called *adhidaivika* [acts of god].

There are hundreds of types of pain: the pain women experience during pregnancy and childbirth; during life we deal with ignorance; then, facing old age, we fear our coming death and the notion of hell. Preparing for our next birth, while in utero, we suffer as a result of having a delicate body surrounded by impurities. The fetus is wrapped in a membrane (amniotic sac), and [is] crumpled and cramped by one's own bones. The mother's diet causes extreme discomfort to the fetus. The conscious fetus is in great sorrow over this bondage, which was created by the karma of previous lifetimes as this cycle repeats over and over again. And when the child is born it is surrounded by impurities and violently pushed by intense labor pains (*prajapatya vayu*). It is a painful process for both the mother and the newborn. Coming into contact with the outside world, the baby immediately forgets its past lifetimes. The child is unable to do anything

> on its own, not even turn over, and is absolutely dependent. As the child is overwhelmed by ignorance (*ajnana*), it is unable to comprehend from where it came, who it is, or where it is going. It does not know what is right (*dharma*) and what is wrong (*adharma*). In what state am I in?"

This passage informs us that pain and sorrow occur not only during life, but even while we're in the womb. Further with this ignorance, the child, as it grows, has to learn again from scratch, and most go through learning pains—yes, many students find school and study painful. Some get the required knowledge, but many suffer from continued ignorance.

The way people have gone about trying to remove suffering needs to be investigated (*jijnasa*). Let us strive to discover a permanent means of eradicating suffering and the cause of suffering definitively, which is to say once and for all.

Many texts start with the word *atha*, "auspiciousness." But the Samkhya Karika starts with the word *duhkha*, "pain," "sorrow." If we eliminate duhkha, what results is auspiciousness, hence the author, Ishvarakrishna, starts out with duhkha. The word *duhkha* can be split into two parts: *du* + *kham du* = something vitiated or bad. *Kham* is "space," referring not to physical space, but to the mental space (*cittaakasa*) that is vitiated. Hence duhkha is vitiated or impaired mental space.

As Krishnamacharya notes in the passage quoted above, there are three types of duhkha: *adhyatmika*, *adhibhautika*, and *adhidaivika*.

1. *Adhyatmika duhkha* is caused by oneself and refers to problems created in the body such as illness. It is created by oneself within oneself, and only the individual person suffers because of it, others do not suffer. This is further divided into physical ailments (*vyadhi*) and mental ailments (*adhi*).

2. ***Adhibhautika duhkha*** is caused by other beings, including other people.

3. ***Adhidaivika duhkha*** is caused by "acts of God," i.e., by *devas*, subtle nature beings or gods. When we do not propitiate the nature beings or gods by acting in harmony with nature, nature becomes enraged. When the earth god becomes enraged, earthquakes result; when the winds or air element/god becomes enraged, tornadoes result. The same with the other natural elements under different minor gods. Every aspect of nature can create problems. According to the scriptures, we should maintain balance by propitiating these nature beings or devas/gods.

According to Indian mythology (as found in the Puranas), when the Lord created the universe, He did not want to micromanage the universe with so many varied factors such as wind and fire. So, he created gods or devas to manage these. It is said that there are 330 million gods managing the Lord's enterprise. Gods or devas are there for truth, speech, and even anger and love. He decreed that the human beings who benefit from the bounty given by the gods of nature should appropriately recognize the gods and worship them through ritualistic offerings, lest they become angry and create huge problems through chaotic behavior by nature. So it is from that perspective we have to interpret the term *adhidaivika*, or acts of the gods.

Yoga students will find that Patanjali looks at the categorization of the three types of duhkha somewhat differently. He describes the three types of suffering as change (*parinama*), anxiety or restlessness (*tapa*), and deeply rooted habits (*samskara*).

What is parinama duhkha, the suffering caused by change? Everything changes in nature, which is of the world of form known as *prakriti*. Seventeenth-century English poet John Wilmot wrote, "Since it's nature's law to change, constancy alone is strange." The exception to this, as we shall see, is the seer, the witness, or the Self, known as *purusha*. What appears good at any given moment may become harmful later as the object changes. The loving couple divorce after seven years as one or both change. Life is a rollercoaster. There is always an apprehension in good times that things will change unfavorably.

The second cause of suffering is *tapa*, which comes from the root *tap*, "to heat." The person in tapa feels like a cat on a hot tin roof (nothing to do with the classic play). One is restless and anxious. This is mentioned in the Taittiriya Upanishad: "All human beings, nay, all creatures, mainly work to get what one wants [*pravritti*] and get rid of what one does not want [*nivritti*]."* A well-known example is found in Vedanta: When a cow is shown a basketful of grass, it comes close to the giver. Conversely, when that same person raises a stick, the cow runs away from the offender. Our lives are always dominated by these two goals—getting what we want and avoiding or getting rid of what we don't want. However, many times, even with the best effort, one does not get what one wants and equally is unable to get rid of what one doesn't want. This Upanishad beautifully pictures the state of the mind of one in a state of tapa. The poor one working hard, unable to make both ends meet and in a state of suffering, laments, "What good deeds have I not done to be rich and comfortable in life?" On the other hand, another person, otherwise rich and famous, suffers from an incurable disease and laments, "What bad deeds or karma have I done to suffer like this, unable to eradicate this ailment?"

Then there is samskara duhkha. Some people are habitually in a state of sorrow or depression. Some children sulk, and the more they sulk, the more unhappy they become, and this can become a habit. Later in life, as adults these people may have

---

*The Sanskrit transliteration is *Yesham ha va vana tapati'/ Kim aham sadhu na akaravam / Kim aham papam akaravam iti.*

difficulty finding happiness even when they are otherwise rich, famous, and successful. Furthermore, it is common knowledge that bad actions lead to painful results. A sensible person may try to eschew such actions, but due to samskaras—habitual actions or behavior—they may have difficulty avoiding such activities as drinking in excess or smoking cigarettes, addictions that are difficult to overcome.

Duhkha produces suffering and pain (*ghatah*). We are constantly trying to eliminate duhkha. Having repeatedly experienced suffering, there is a desire in us to know (*jijnasa*) the means by which we will be able to eliminate duhkha and completely destroy its causes.

Here is an objection, this sloka points out: All the means are known to us already, and so this desire is pointless. But in reply it is said that all the solutions that are already known to us suffer from two obstacles. What are they?

1. We do not have a definitive solution (*eikantata*), meaning the same solution or method does not work every time and for everybody.

2. The permanency (*atyantata*) of any solution eludes us, meaning any solution is temporary at best.

The goal of Samkhya is to remove duhkha permanently and definitively. Can I go through life without duhkha, even though the circumstances that create suffering continue to exist? Equally or more importantly, can I avoid the suffering that will come with future births, or rather can I avoid a future birth?

Most people do not mind tons of duhkha and are happy with a few crumbs of happiness. But sages, according to the rishi Veda Vyasa, who classified the Vedas, are like eyeballs. The eyeball is so sensitive that it cannot tolerate even a small speck of dust, unlike the skin of your arms and legs. These sages look at the never-ending duhkha of most people who act as though they are chasing a will-o'-the-wisp. Maybe the truth proclaimed by the wise ones will appeal to a few equally sensitive and sensible ones. Certainly, there were a few in the olden days who would sacrifice worldly pleasures for the heavens they could reach in the hereafter, by following dharmas such as are found in Vedic scriptures like the brahmana portions and by practicing the rituals outlined in these ancient texts. The next sloka finds fault with even the approach of going to the heavens. It has its own shortcomings.

Kārikā 2

> Known means of eliminating suffering are defective, so are the heavenly pursuits. The principles of Samkhya provide the only remedy.

दृष्टवदानुश्रविकः स ह्यविशुद्धिक्षयातिशययुक्तः ।
तद्विपरीतःश्रेयान्व्यक्ताव्यक्तज्ञविज्ञानात् ॥ २॥

Dṛṣṭavadānuśravikaḥsa hyaviśuddhi1 kṣayātiśayayuktaḥ |
tadviparītaḥśreyānvyaktāvyaktajñavijñānāt ||2||

dṛṣṭavat—like something that is seen, the worldly means
ānuśravikaḥ—Vedic rituals (also are defective)
aviśuddhi—impure
kshaya—depleting
atisayayuktaḥ—associated with being surpassed
tadviparītaḥ—that which is different from these known solutions
śreyān—superior

vyakta—manifest
avyakta—source or unmanifest
jñah—consciousness, awareness, the Self
vijñānāt—understanding thoroughly

// The means mentioned in the first sloka are defective; likewise, the Vedic rituals are also defective because they are impure, impermanent due to depleting virtue (*punya*), and also surpassed. To be free of duhkha is to have the knowledge of the manifest universe, the source of the universe, and the nature of the knower or consciousness. //

The means of eliminating suffering suggested by Vedic rituals are defective solutions. They are defective because of the following:

1. They are impure (*avisuddhi*). All religious activities are not completely pure (*sattvic*). For example, when we do a fire offering to the various gods for fulfilling some out of the world and hereafter benefits (kamya karmas), we use a lot of resources for the offering, which deprives other people or creatures of those essential resources. Even though we may ultimately get what we want, it is with a tinge of sin (*papa*), it is said. For example, in the old days, the king who wanted to become emperor would consider performing an Aswamedha ritual, the famous horse sacrifice ritual of ancient times. This required mobilizing enormous resources. The king would tax his subjects to the hilt to pay for a huge army and weapons. Then he would release one of his thoroughbreds to wander through neighboring countries accompanied by the king's warriors. After a period of time, if no one managed to kill or capture the horse by defeating his army surrounding the horse, the animal would be returned to the king's capital, whereupon it would then be sacrificed and the king declared emperor. Of course, many orthodox pandits would say that there is no sin that would accrue from this since it is a Vedic ritual (in ancient times; it is no longer performed), even though it entails cruelty and pain caused to humans and animals. But causing pain is bad karma. So here samkhyas take the view that these karmas are unclean, as they cause pain and thus violate the basic principle of *ahimsa*, do no harm.

2. There is always something higher that we are reaching for (*atisaya*). For example, if you are a millionaire, you compare your status with a multimillionaire or billionaire. There are many heavens. When you reach one you see the higher levels of heaven and you may feel less happy by comparing where you're at with something higher that you haven't achieved yet. The Puranas mention seven heavens, and I understand that there are about four hundred or so mentioned in the Vedas. The Taittiriya Upanishad, in driving home the unsurpassed bliss that can arise out of brahmanhood, refers to the many heavens that afford increasing levels of happiness. Life on earth gives its own happiness, but it is extremely limited. Let's imagine the happiest person—such a person would be young, as youth affords its own measure of happiness. This young person is also pious, as well as a scholar of the Vedas and hence very knowledgeable. Knowledge gives its own happiness. Well-behaved, with all physical abilities functioning well, and very strong, too. He is vastly propertied and endowed with riches. Let us consider his happiness as one unit of human happiness. No human being can be happier than him. All others have less happiness and more unhappiness compared to our ideal human being. But then the happiness one can experience as a celestial being (*manushya gandharva*) or semicelestial being (a human *gandharva*) is one hundred times more joyful than what a human being can possibly experience, says this Upanishad. But a hundred times more happiness would accrue, it is said, if one can become a deva gandharva, a semidivine celestial being. And there are even more levels.

One hundred times happier than a deva gandharva would be the one who by good karma enters the long-lasting *pitru loka*, the astral plane where virtuous souls go to enjoy their good karma. Then the divine beings in high heaven are a hundred times happier than those in the pitru loka. A hundred times happier still would be those devic beings who reach heaven due to the righteous deeds they performed according to the scriptures. One hundred times happier still are those devas who accept offerings in rituals. And the boss of the devas, Indra, is said to be a hundred times happier than the devas in the heaven of the devas (*devaloka*). The world of the fire ritual god, Brihaspati, gives a hundred times more happiness than that of Indra himself. Brahaspati is the celestial priest, the enormously wise one teaching even the divine ones. And the world of Prajapati, the great creator diety of the Vedas, is even more blissful by a hundred times. And the world of Chaturmukha Brahma is a hundred times more blissful than the world of Prajapati.

Of course, the purpose of this Upanishad passage is to show that even as the higher worlds offer higher and higher degrees of happiness, the unsurpassed infinite bliss arises only from knowledge of Brahman and complete liberation (*moksha* or *kaivalya*) that those who follow the path of Samkhya, Yoga, or Vedanta strive to achieve.

So here samkhyas say that compared to the higher heavens, entities in the lower heavens feel unhappiness, duhkha. We see a poor man is unhappy compared to a well-to-do person. A well-to-do person feels a tinge of unhappiness when comparing himself to a millionaire. The millionaire is concerned that he is not a multimillionaire like his unfriendly neighbor. Then there is the billionaire who creates jealousy in the mind of a multimillionaire . . . and so on.

3. The accumulation of virtue gets used up (*kshaya*). One therefore has to go "back to the drawing board" to collect fresh karma and experience the effects of past unripened karmas. The law of karma always catches up with us. Here is a story that illustrates this:

There was once a king who wanted to become an emperor. He performed the Aswamedha ritual and was subsequently able to dominate many neighboring countries. He became emperor. After that he was told that if he would do a hundred horse sacrifice rituals, he would become Indra, the boss of the gods. Thereafter he did a hundred horse sacrifice rituals and conquered all the world in the universe. In the course of time, he died. His subtle body went all the way to heaven, Indra's heaven. He was crowned Indra on account of having performed the hundred horse sacrifice rituals. As soon as he became Indra, he wanted to completely change all of heaven because he thought, *No, no, this heaven should be better. There should be four towers.* So, he called the divine architect, Vishvakarma, and drove him crazy asking him to do this, do that, and completely modify the palace and heaven itself. Vishvakarma did everything ordered by the new Indra, but he became disgusted. He went out and sat down under a tree and did not report for duty for a day.

At that time there was a sage who passed by and saw Vishvakarma sitting under the tree. The sage asked him, "What is the problem? You look so distraught, very unlike your cheerful self."

"This new Indra is crazy," said the heavenly builder. "He is not only crazy; he is driving me crazy."

"What happened?" the sage asked. After listening to Vishvakarma's sob story, the sage thought that what the architect said was right—a little bit of an adjustment is good, but complete change it is not going to be good, it is purposeless. *Let me go talk to Indra*, thought the sage.

He went to the Lord of Heaven, who was very happy that the great sage came to see him after he'd achieved the best possible position in the whole universe. The sage talked to the new Indra for a few minutes and asked how he was enjoying his new status. Indra said, "You know, I am not very happy. We should change all of heaven, completely modernize it." Just at that time, an army of ants started to come out into the palace through a small crevice. The sage pointed the ants out to Indra and asked, "Do you see these ants?"

"Yes, of course I see the ants," said the unhappy Indra. Immediately, he became angry and muttered, "Okay, I will call Vishvakarma to completely close up all the holes in the palace. I don't like this." He called the heavenly builder, and Vishvakarma came to him, and immediately Indra started shouting at him. The sage interjected and said, "No, no, the reason why I wanted you to see the ants was not so you could shout at Vishvakarma. I wanted to tell you something else that is important. How many ants did you see?"

"About a hundred of them, I guess," the new Indra replied.

"All these one hundred ants were Indras before this. They were all Indras. After their good karma was over, they fell down and had to continue to experience the effects of their accumulated but unfruitful previous karma."

In this way the sage was able to put some sense into the head of the new Indra. The erstwhile king finally sobered and understood that what he had acquired was temporary.

So, *kshaya* means that when you go to heaven, it is not permanent. You may be there for a particular yuga, but when dissolution takes place, you are on par with any other creature, left with your own residual karmas. If you use up all your good karma, after that you will fall down. Trying to go to heaven is not a permanent escape from duhkha—that's the whole idea.

When I was young, there were very few houses around my house, and we used to enjoy vast open space. I used to gaze at the night sky once in a while, and I would see a meteor or some shiny object stream down from the sky and disappear. My grandmother had a story about this phenomenon. She would say that a person who had gone to a higher world due to good karmas was falling down after the benefits of their virtue had been exhausted.

Knowledge of the following will help you achieve something superior, something different from the feeling of duhkha. When we understand these things, we are able to achieve a mental state that is higher and different from the one we had before. There will be what Patanjali calls *citta vritti nirodha*—the cessation of the various activities of the mind, or yoga.

What are the three things one should know?

- ***vyakta***, the manifest universe
- ***avyakta***, the unmanifest source of the universe
- ***jnah***, the knower; consciousness, the Self, the subject

Here Ishvarakrishna is saying that one should know how the universe evolved, the source of the universe, and finally and most importantly, the nature of the subject who is aware of the objects of reality.

Kārikā 3

Purusha and prakriti as the philosophical foundation of Samkhya and the nuanced evolution of the objective universe

मूलप्रकृतिरविकृतिर्महदाद्याः प्रकृतिविकृतयःसप्त ।
षोडशकस्तुविकारो न प्रकृतिर्नविकृतिःपुरुषः ॥ ३ ॥

Mūlaprakṛtiravikṛtirmahadādyāḥ prakṛtivikṛtayaḥsapta
ṣoḍaśakastuvikāronaprakṛtirnavikṛtiḥpuruṣaḥ ||3||

mūlaprakruti—the absolute source of the universe
avikṛtiḥ—is not a product of something
mahataadyaah—greatest principle (universal intelligence) and others
prakriti vikritayah—those that produce another and are themselves products
sapta—are seven in number
vikarah—the stand-alone evolutes
shodakah—are sixteen in number
purushah—the indwelling Self mentioned as awareness (*jnah*) in the previous sloka
na prakritih vikritih—is neither a product nor does it produce anything

// Mulaprakriti and purusha are not products of something else, whereas twenty-three of the twenty-five tattvas are the products of something, and seven in turn are also capable of producing something. Sixteen tattvas are produced but are incapable of producing something else. Purusha is the one tattva that is neither prakriti nor vikriti; it does not produce anything, nor is it a product of something. //

In this sloka, Ishvarakrishna explains the two principles that form the basis of the philosophy of Samkhya, prakriti, and purusha. In so doing, this karika elaborates on the nature of the universe and how it evolves, as follows:

Objects and entities that are manifest forms (vykata) are produced from manifest forms and themselves are capable of producing other entities.

The unmanifest (avyakta), pre-cosmic root substance, mulaprakriti, is the source of the universe. This source is not a product of something; there is nothing that is the source of mulaprakriti, but it produces something. While prakriti is capable of creating and can be a producer of something other than itself, mulaprakriti refers to the original source of the universe (as yoga students know, *mula* means "root"), that is, the absolute source of the evolved universe, which is unmanifest. It exists, but we cannot say where it exists. Its effects can be further seen in the form of the three qualities, or *gunas*: goodness and positivity (*sattva*), energy and activity (*rajas*), and limitations and restrictions (*tamas*).

Universal or cosmic intelligence (mahat) is capable of order in the creation of the universe. In other words, the universe is not a random creation. Because it is universal or cosmic intelligence, it creates and maintains the universe in a particular order.

From cosmic intelligence (mahat) emerges the ego (ahamkara) and the principle of individuation. From this emerges the five sense organs: the eyes, ears, skin, tongue, and nose. Then the five organs of action manifest: the legs, arms, voice, generative organs, and excretory organ. Then there are the five elements of earth, water, fire, air, and space arising out of sensations of the five senses (*tanmatras*)—light, sound, taste, smell, and tactile sensation.

Consciousness (jnah) is the essence of the purusha and is neither a product of something else, nor does it produce something. It is immortal, permanent, and eternal, without undergoing any changes whatsoever. It is called the Self, the seer, the knower, the indweller, awareness, consciousness, and the power of experiencing.

The Vedic philosophies or schools are six in number, as mentioned earlier, and ancient scholars like my guru Sri Krishnamacharya were proficient in all the schools, but particularly in Samkhya, Yoga, and Vedanta, the three philosophies that have the goal of enabling the practitioner to prevent future rebirths and the suffering those entail. Even as there are significant differences among these three schools, especially between the Samkhya/Yoga duo and Vedanta, these three siblings have one thing in common, and that concerns the nature of the Self. They all aver that the true Self is pure, unvarying consciousness, and so it is a mistake (Shankaracharya calls it *anartha*, a hindrance) to consider the physical body-mind complex as the Self, a common misunderstanding. The Self is pure, unvarying consciousness. Vedic philosophy explains in considerable detail this rather important but not literally apparent fact. The distinction (what is called *viveka*, "discrimination") between the Self (purusha) and the physically incarnate self or physical matter in general (prakriti) is the main theme of all three of these Vedic schools.

The Bhagavad Gita, from the great epic the Mahabharata, is an ancient epic, or *itihasa*, that is still studied in great depth today.* It deals with an issue that many people throughout time can relate to. In it, the advice given by the Lord to Arjuna deals with the nature of conflict.

Many of us find ourselves in the situation Arjuna was in. Property disputes of different magnitudes and disputes among siblings, cousins, and other relatives are common all over the world. Some people fight hard, some give up early; some are emotionally drained from fighting with one's own kith and kin. Many times, people who've been caught up in such situations go for advice from elders or professionals. In the case of Arjuna, he was fighting a just cause, but was distraught as he had to fight his cousins, uncles, revered teachers, and even a beloved grandfather. That was when Lord Krishna stepped in to advise Arjuna

*The Mahabharata consists of over 100,000 slokas, or couplets, and is considered the longest known epic poem; by comparison it is ten times the combined length of Homer's *Illiad* and *Odyssey*.

about the right thing to do, to fight or to give up the fight—not because Arjuna was incapable of fighting, but because of the emotional strain on him. Many of us can sympathize with Arjuna's predicament, as he was fighting for dharma.

The first and foremost message that the Lord gives Arjuna concerns the nature of the individual Self, or atman. He declares that all creatures are essentially immortal. This instruction about the atman, which you can find in Samkhya, Yoga, and Vedanta, is usually given to renunciates, yogis, and maybe to retirees, but not to a warrior in the battlefield right before the start of a war. By talking about the nature of the atman, the Lord was able to lay the foundation for subsequent reasonings he would put forward. But the thing to note here is that quite possibly the Lord would not have been able to convince Arjuna to do the right thing without imparting knowledge of the Self.

And what is the nature of the Self, the atman? It is pure, unvarying, immortal consciousness. It is that which experiences what every person is said to experience. How do we experience the outside world? My school science teacher would ask, "How do you see?" and we would reply, "With our eyes." He would then say that the eyes do not have consciousness. They are just a sense organ that captures the light particles emanated from objects and transmits to the brain as electrical impulses through the optical nerve system. "It is the brain that sees," he would then say.

"No, the brain has no consciousness, it cannot see," would be the chorus of samkhyas, yogis, and vedantins in response. Yogis point out that the brain, which they call *citta*, is prakritic, organic matter. Why so? How does the brain evolve? The sperm has no consciousness to experience, nor do the egg or the embryo. Further development beyond this stage into a fetus happens with the addition of food through the mother, but this food is not capable of experiencing as we do. The brain, that part of a human being made up of fats and lipids, *appears* to have consciousness though. The term *citta* describes the brain, and its activities are called *cittavrittis*, while the word *cit* refers more specifically to consciousness. Distinguishing between these two, my guru would say, "*Cit iva bhavayati it cittam*," "That which masquerades as having consciousness is *citta*." And because of the inability of the aspirant to distinguish between these two, *cit* and *citta*, there is the mistaken impression that the brain, or *citta*, has consciousness.

The great Shankaracharya takes up the discussion of the difference between the subject and the object in order to deduce the nature of the subject, or what should be called the "I," in his preamble to the Brahma Sutra Bhashya, the fundamental text of the Vedanta school. The following example illustrates this principle:

You and I are sitting across a table from each other having a cup of coffee. From my perspective I am the subject and you are the object. We are both distinctly different, as different as day and night. Our personal characteristics are even more varied. That being the case, how can one not see the difference between the subject, which is the experiencer, and the object, the objective world outside of the experiencer? What does the subject experience at this moment? I experience not only the outside world, but also myself, a 150-pound, eighty-five-year-old man, including the brain of this man, which is the object being experienced. The totality of my experience is the object. What is it that is experienced? You sitting in front of me, the other surrounding objects, and also me, Ramaswami, sitting and conversing with you. The subject in this case would be the Self, the seer, which is pure unvarying consciousness. But how is it that we confuse the nonself with the Self? When did this confusion arise? There has been no beginning to this confusion; it has been with us lifetime after lifetime. But there is an end to it, and that's when we finally realize the nature of the Self. Take the case of an infant abandoned by parents and brought up by adoptive parents. At a later adult stage, the child may come to know that the adoptive parents are not his or her biological parents, and with that the longstanding notion that they are the birth parents is suddenly gone with this new perspective.

Can we have a more detailed discussion? Let's get back to our science teacher. We agree with him that the eyes, ears, and other senses have no consciousness but are sensitive to specific stimuli. But when these electrical impulses from the sensory organs stimulated by the external stimuli like light particles or sound waves reach the brain, they have to be processed and then converted into images that we then perceive. The brain receives regular impulses from the physical senses through the complex nervous system, which is part of the process. The brain then projects a composite image that includes the emotions and all. Since this composite image includes myself, this physical "I" is also part of what is being experienced. Thus, yogis call the totality of what is experienced in any given moment *cittavritti*, while that which experiences is pure unvarying consciousness, the subject, the seer, the experiencer, or *jnah*, as samkhyas say, or the *drashta* as yogis would say. It is significant that Patanjali uses the term *drashta*, or seer, indicating that the eyes do not see, nor does the brain or *citta*; it is the Self, the *drashta*, the purusha, that is the seer. A moment's reflection would show that one's consciousness does not change, in fact never changes, even as experiences change from moment to moment. If one is able to slowly start considering consciousness as the Self, the true "I," we will realize a certain peace, as the Self is immutable, immortal, and needs no special attention because in time, with this realization, the practitioner will attain liberation. All our activities are for the sake of ourselves, but when the subject, which is pure consciousness, is unaffected by good or bad experiences, the mind or intellect of the person will cease to operate the way it had been functioning, in confusion.

So, one might conclude from this that the disciplines of Samkhya, Yoga, and Vedanta are for sanyasins, yogis, and those with similar dispositions—in other words, they are useful only for a very few. No, Lord Krishna would say. The Bhagavad Gita is addressed not to a scholar, nor to a renunciate or a yogi; it is addressed to an ordinary warrior in a state of utter dismay and confusion, like most of us are. The fundamental instruction is to know the nature of the Self. It implies that if ordinary people like us had knowledge of the Self as articulated in the shastras and as expounded by the Lord, it would greatly lessen the burden human beings carry in their minds. The Lord advises Arjuna to always keep in mind an understanding of the nature of the Self; one should do one's duty and fulfill one's responsibilities, but not be overly concerned about the physical or prakritic person as it is the non-self. It is said in the Bhagavad Gita,

योगस्थः कुरु कर्माणि सङ्गं त्यक्त्वा धनञ्जय ।

yogastha: kuru karmāṇi saṅgaṃtyaktvā dhanañjaya |

With the *buddhi* (the intellect) in unison with the atman (the Self), do your duty without attachment to the empirical or to what is seen.

There are many instances throughout history when people with enormous responsibilities would carry them out while at the same time having knowledge of the Self (*atmajnana*), like the Hindu king Janaka, the sage Yajnyavalkya, or the scholar Shankaracharya. This suggests that knowledge of the Self through the disciplines of Samkhya, Yoga, and Vedanta—or even just the Gita alone—should be imparted early in life. Even knowledge of just part of chapter 2 of the Gita would be helpful. The Lord advised Arjuna on what he should do if he wins the war in Kurukshtra: he should eschew worldly pursuits (*sarva arambha parityagi*) and instead become a yogi (*tasmat yogi bhavarjuna*). Atmajnana, or knowledge of the Self, can be imparted early in life, yet many people don't start studying this wisdom until after they've retired and are in old age.

The eyes do not see
The brain does not see
The purusha sees
Thus, it is called seer or drashta.

The one who thoroughly knows all the twenty-five tattvas, the aspects of human reality, becomes free, says a famous sloka. And what are the twenty-five tattvas?

1. Purusha (Self; pure, unvarying consciousness; immortal; the subject)
2. Mulaprakriti (the source of the universe possessing the three gunas in perfect equilibrium)
3. Mahat, buddhi (cosmic intelligence and universal order, sattvic evolute, individual intellect)
4. Ahamkara (cosmic energy, individual ego, motivator to act)
5. Manas (mind, coordinates all the instruments of action and the senses, like eye-hand coordination, etc.)

6–10. Jnanendriyas (the five sense organs—eyes, ears, nose, tongue, skin)

11–15. Karmendriyas (the five motor organs—mouth, feet, hands, genitals, anus)

16–20. Tanmatras (the five subtle elements or sensations—light, sound, taste, smell, touch)

21–25. Pancha bhutas (the five gross elements—earth, water, fire, air, space)

Kārikā 4

The means of proof of Samkhya philosophy and its underlying concepts of prakriti and purusha

दृष्टमनुमानमाप्तवचनं च सर्वप्रमाणसिद्धत्वात् ।
त्रिविधंप्रमाणमिष्टंप्रमेयसिद्धिःप्रमाणाद्धि ॥ ४॥

Dṛṣṭamanumānamāptavacanaṃ ca sarvapramāṇasiddhatvāt |
trividhaṃpramāṇamiṣṭaṃprameyasiddhiḥpramāṇāddhi ||4||

dṛṣṭam—direct perception through the five senses
anumāna—inference
aptavacanam ca—testimony from a person who is trustworthy and knowledgeable
sarvapramanasidhyatvat—for the sake of knowing all the objects
pramāṇam—means of knowing the truth, proofs
trividham—three types
iṣṭam—it is agreed by philosophers
prameyasiddhih—knowing the objects is achieved
hi—surely, only by
pramanat—from proofs or by the right sources of knowledge

// To attain the right knowledge (*pramanam*) of all twenty-five tattvas, or principles of reality, followers of Samkhya employ three means. The first is direct perception through the senses (*drastam*). Then there is inference (*anumana*). Finally, there are the words of like-minded knowledgeable dear friends (*aptavacanam*). You will be able to understand the truth of

the various principles, or tattvas, only by these means. All philosophers agree on this. //

Vedic philosophies are quite scientific in that they take a practical, systematic approach to finding the proofs, as is evident in Samkhya philosophy. Knowing the nature of the Self, the source of the universe, and the evolution of the universe requires more than mere sensory perception. In any scientific inquiry as well as in Samkhya, inference also plays an important role. Hence the ground is prepared for knowing the truth about the knower of all (*jnah*), the pre-cosmic, unmanifest source of the universe (*mulaprakriti*), and its myriad evolutes (*prakriti*) that manifest as objects and entities. Here Ishvarakrishna tells us how to know the truth as found in Samkhya philosophy:

- ***Pramana,*** proof, implies a method for understanding the truth. Once we know that we want to understand the truth, we must have the means to do so.
- ***Prameya*** is the object whose truth we want to understand.
- ***Pramatru*** is the person who wants to understand the truth.

These three are called the *triputis*, which means "the three aspects of obtaining knowledge." This compares with Patanjali's similar delineation of the triputis as *grahitru*, "the cognizer"; *grahana*, "cognition"; and *graha*, "cognized object."

According to Samkhya philosophy, there are three methods of apprehending the truth:

Truth can be directly perceived through the senses (drstam). For example, the five elements of earth, air, fire, water, and space can be experienced through one of the five physical sense organs. This is known as *pratyaksha*, and in Yoga philosophy it means "that which is right in front of your eyes (or perceived by the other senses)."

Truth can be inferred (anumana) by what is perceived by the senses and retained in the memory to be recalled as an inference.

Some things cannot be known directly or even inferred, for instance the nature of the true Self. But we can know the truth of such things through the testimony (*aptavacanam*) of a person or authority in whom we have faith and who is knowledgeable, such as a sage or a respected teacher. Patanjali uses the term *agama*, "scriptures," to refer to such a source when talking about realizing the Self, or atman.

Kārikā 5

The three types of proofs—direct perception, inference, and valid testimony

प्रतिविषयाध्यवसायोदृष्टं त्रिविधमनुमानमाख्यातम्।
तल्लिङ्गलिङ्गि२पूर्वकमाप्तश्रुतिराप्तवचनं तु ॥ ५॥

Prativiṣayādhyavasāyodṛṣṭaṃtrividhamanumānamākhyātam |
talliṅgaliṅgipūrvakamāptaśrutirāptavacanaṃtu ||5||

prativiṣaya—every object
adhyavasāyah—going deep into, using the senses, being totally attentive
drishtam—is direct perception
anumana—inference
trividam—is of three types
akhyatam—it is known to be
tat—that

anumana—inference
lingalingipurvakam—an object (*lingi*) is known from symptoms or clues (*linga*)
aptasrutih—scriptures
tu—surely
aptavakyam—are trusted sayings (on matters dealt with by samkhyas, yogis, and vedantins)

// Direct perception (*drishtam*) is when the senses are completely focused on their respective objects (*adhyavasaya*, "to plow through thoroughly"). Inference (*anumana*) is based on the relationship between an entity and the symptoms it exhibits (*lingalingipurvakam*). Inference is of three types: inference derived from a similar previous experience (*purvavat*), inference that derives a cause from its effect (*sesavat*), and inference as a result of having a common characteristic (*samanyavat*). //

Every sense organ has an object (*vishaya*) of cognition. The object of cognition for the eyes is light; for the ears it is sound; for the tongue it is taste; for the nose it is smell; and for the skin it is touch. When the senses are completely focused on an object, it is called direct perception (*drishtam*).

For inference to take place there must be some preexisting knowledge gained through direct perception, as well as the application of the knowledge of cause and effect. Inference is of three types:

1. Something has happened before that we have seen, and when the same thing occurs again, we can infer that the same result will happen. This is called *purvavat*, "like the previous one," which is to infer effect from similar cause. For example, when we see dark clouds, we can infer that it will rain. Why? We have seen it rain when there were dark clouds.

2. The cause of something is inferred from its effect. This is called *sesavat*, "like the subsequent one or the remainder." If there is a group of things and we take one sample and analyze that, we can make conclusions about the whole group. For example, you can check a grain of rice to see if all the rice in the pot is cooked. In fact, modern statistical analysis and sampling techniques and the resultant conclusions belong to this group. It allows us to get the correct knowledge of the group and then make appropriate decisions based on that sample.

3. Common observation (*samanyavat*) can tell us that we can arrive at an inference based on commonly observed connections between phenomenon that can be applied to other cases. For example, death is a common occurrence; many have died, so everyone will die. We can therefore conclude that death—as well as taxes—are certain.

Worldly objects are usually known mostly by direct perception using the five senses. If this is not possible, then one may have to infer based on the limited information or clues available. When one is clueless, the only remaining way is to believe the words of a well-meaning and competent, trusted friend. In matters spiritual, where the senses are of no help, the ultimate truth will have to be known first from the scriptures (*agama*). Samkhyas say that the awareness (*jnah*) that is present in each being is aware of objects. That awareness is unchanging and immortal. Anyone, such as the reader, by going through this text will have a knowledge of the Self, an indirect one. That would be pramana or right knowledge through aptavacanam or valid testimony.

In his Yoga Sutras, Patanjali affirms that all the thoughts and activities in one's brain are known due to the unchanging awareness of the indwelling pure consciousness principle that is purusha. This can be confirmed by serious students who follow the logic and thought processes of the sages of old. Then finally, as a result of deep concentration or yogic samadhi, one will be able to directly experience truth. This direct perception is called *yougika pratyakha*, "direct perception by yoga," also known as spiritual perception, as opposed to perception by the senses. *Yougika* means "of yoga." Here one gets information first from the scriptures; then gets it confirmed by deep contemplation; and finally, through yogic discipline, one's intellect, or buddhi, directly perceives the Self in a state of samadhi.

Kārikā 6

Scriptures and testimony as a means of gaining knowledge

सामान्यतस्तुदृष्टादतीन्द्रियाणां प्रतीतिर१नुमानात् ।
तस्मादपिचासिद्धंपरोऽक्षमाप्तागमात् सिद्धं२ ॥ ६॥

Sāmānyatastudṛṣṭādatīndriyāṇāṃpratītirasnumānāt
tasmādapicāsiddhaṃparo'kṣamāptāgamātsiddhaṃ ||6||

tu—surely
sāmānyata tu dṛṣṭāt—ordinarily things that can be known are known through the senses
atīndriyāṣām—objects beyond the range of the senses
prasiddhiḥ—are known conclusively
anumānāt—only through inference
tasmādapi asiddham—those that are not understood even through it or by inference
parokṣam—through some other means which is
aptāgamāt—appropriate part of the Vedas
siddham—are realized

// Proofs (*pramana*) of some objects can be had through direct perception by the senses (*drsta pramana*); and by inference, when the objects are beyond the senses (*anumana pramana*). But when objects are beyond the senses and even inference is not possible, one can gain knowledge through authoritative sources (*paroksham*). //

We ordinarily use direct perception through our senses (*drsta pramana*) to gain knowledge, while anything outside the range of our directly sensing it becomes known to us only by inference (*anumana*), although even in the case of inference some amount of information should be available to the senses. This sloka says that anything that is not known through either of these two means, direct perception or inference, can be known only secondhand, through a recognized authority. This is called *paroksham*, the words of other people, or literally, "through someone else's eyes." While the words of a trusted friend or source (*aptavacanam*) would be a third option in the case of worldly matters, for spiritual matters, especially when it comes to knowledge of the Self, one can gain this knowledge in the initial stage, only through scriptures like the Vedas or through *nivritti shastras* like Samkhya.

Kārikā 7

Obstacles to not knowing an object directly or by inference

अतिदूरात्सामीप्यादिन्द्रियघातान्मनोऽनवस्थानात् ।
सौक्ष्म्याद्व्यवधानादभिभवात्समानाभिहाराच्च ॥ ७॥

Atidūrātsāmīpyādindriyaghātānmano'navasthānāt |
saukṣmyādvyavadhānādabhibhavātsamānābhihāracca ||7||

atidūrāt—if far away, beyond the range of perception by the senses
sāmīpyāt—if too close
indriyaghātāt—if senses are injured, impaired
manonavasthānāt—if and when the mind is not focused
saukṣmyāt—if the object is very subtle
vyavadhānāt—if hidden
abhibhāvāt—if when there is something overpowering the object
samānaabhiharāt—if when with other objects that are identical to the object under consideration

// The eight reasons why we are not able to perceive things even as they exist is because they are beyond the range of the senses (*atidurat*); they are too close to the senses (*samipyat*); the senses are impaired (*indriyaghatat*); we cannot focus on the object as the mind is distracted (*manoavasthanat*); the object is too subtle to be perceived (*sauksmyat*); the object is hidden or not discernable (*vyavadhanat*); the object is somehow obscured (*abhibhavat*); and the object can be confused with other similar objects (*samanaabiharat*). //

This sloka talks about the limits of the sensory faculties in knowing the truth of objects, which is a factor in both inference and direct perception. There are many reasons why we are not able to see things that exist. But just because we are not able to see them does not mean they do not exist. The text then explains the eight reasons why we cannot see existing things.

1. When an object is far away, one cannot see it or hear its sound (*atidurat*). The world we live in is a very small portion of the universe. And what we see in the world is a very small part of the world. This is well-known, but it is one important reason why existing objects may not be known. Just because we cannot perceive it, we cannot conclude that the object of inquiry does not exist. Far away objects are not discernable.

2. Objects too close to us also are not seen (*saamipyat*). If you bring an object very close to the eye it cannot be seen, as it will be out of focus.

3. If a sense organ like the eye or the ear is afflicted, objects that can be known only through that particular sense will not be known at all (*indriya ghatat*), yet one cannot conclude that the particular object does not exist. In the olden days the Vedas were only recited but never written. So, the person who was deaf might wrongly conclude that the Vedas do not exist or would be blissfully unaware of the sacred texts.

4. When the mind is unfocused, objects, even when they are grasped by the senses, may not be known even if they do exist (*manoavastanat*). When I am keenly watching a game of cricket or engaged in deep concentration (*ekagrata*), any other stimulus that arises will be unattended by my mind. When the mind is in concentration or samadhi, the yogi becomes completely oblivious to the outside world. In fact, the yogi in a state of samadhi is completely oblivious to his or her own body.

5. Being too subtle (*soukshmyat*) could also be a cause for not apprehending an object. For example, none of the senses is able to recognize viruses, but we cannot say that viruses and bacteria do not exist. We are painfully aware that these unseen organisms exist.

6. When an object is hidden (*vyavadanat*), it cannot be seen. Hidden treasures of the olden days, or hidden unaccounted wealth in modern times are prime examples.

7. When an object is forcibly suppressed (*abhibhavat*), it cannot be seen. The example given by the scholars of old is that the stars that shine brilliantly at night cannot be seen during the day because the sun's rays suppress their visibility. They exist nevertheless and wait for the night to show their glory.

8. When objects look alike or are identical, it is difficult or impossible to identify or distinguish the particular object (*samana abiharat*). A drop of rainwater falls in the ocean; it is impossible to isolate and find that particular drop of water—nor, for that matter, can I distinguish between my wonderful twin grandchildren.

Why does Ishvarakrishna talk about these obstacles to knowledge that are obvious, even to a child? Because a treatise such as this should be complete, and the Vedas stress the importance of arriving at logical, scientific conclusions.

Kārikā 8

Reasons for the nonperception of the cosmic root substance, mulaprakriti

सौक्ष्म्यात्तदनुपलब्धिर्नाभावात्कार्यतस्तदुपलब्धिः ।
महदादि तच्च२ कार्यंप्रकृतिविरूपंसरूपं च ॥ ८॥

Saukṣmyāttadanupalabdhirnābhāvātkāryatastadupalabdhiḥ |
mahadāditaccakāryaṃprakṛtivirūpaṃsarūpaṃ ca ||8||

saukṣmyāt—because of being subtle
tat—that (mulaprakriti)

anupalabdhi—not able to get close to or be experienced
na—not
abhāvāt—because it does not exist (*abhava* means "nonexistence")
kāryataḥ—from its effect
tat upalabdhi—one can infer that
mahat, mahat tattva—the greatest, the cosmic intelligence
ādi—and others
kāryam—are its effects and further
prakriti—the cause
sarupamvirupam ca—similar to and different from

// Because the root cause of all phenomena, mulaprakriti, is subtle, we are not able to get close to it, but not because it does not exist. We can infer its existence from its effects or its evolutes. Importantly, these evolutes have similarities as well as differences with the root cause. //

This sloka says that the root cause of all phenomena, mulaprakriti, exists, but we are not able to find it because of one of the eight reasons mentioned in the previous sloka. Which one? Because mulaprakriti is very subtle, we cannot get close to it or even experience it, but that doesn't mean it doesn't exist.

There are four types of nonexistence (*abhava*) according to Vedanta:

1. Something that is going to occur in the future but does not exist now or earlier (*prag abhava*), like my great-grandchild or me achieving liberation

2. Something that existed earlier but does not exist now (*pradvamsa abhava*), for example, all those who are dead and gone

3. Something that cannot exist when a particular space is occupied by something else (*anyonya abhava*), or two things that are mutually exclusive. For example, two people cannot occupy the same space, or where there is light there cannot be darkness.

4. Something that never existed (*atyanta abhava*), for example, the horns of a rabbit

We can infer the existence of mulaprakriti from its effects, which include, as one example, the intellect (*mahat*). The cause of the effect known as the intellect is mulaprakriti, even though mulaprakriti cannot be seen or known. And the intellect is only one of the effects of mulaprakriti. So, though there are various dissimilar effects arising from the unmanifest cosmic root substance that is mulaprakriti, they share the same cause.

How is it that the effects of mulaprakriti can be both similar and different? It's like saying that all men are alike and yet different. The evolutes of mulaprakriti, that is, the forms that arise from it, are similar in that they all exhibit the three qualities (*gunas*): goodness and positivity, or as Ishvarakrishna would say, lightness of the body and clarity of the mind (*sattva*); energy and activity, or as Ishvarakrishna puts it, restlessness at the physical level and fickleness of the mind (*rajas*); and physical limitations and restrictions or heaviness, and being stupified at the mental level (*tamas*). They are different because one of the three gunas will always dominate over the other two to varying degrees, resulting in objects with dissimilar characteristics. This unique, groundbreaking perspective of Samkhya is also shared by Yoga and Vedanta. All objects have the three qualities or gunas, but of a varying mix, which makes for different objects.

Kārikā 9

There is a primary cause for the universe. Because the cause, mulaprakriti, is real, the effect also is real.

असदकरणादुपादानग्रहणात्सर्वसम्भवाभावात् ।
शक्तस्यशक्यकरणात्कारणभावाच्चसत्कार्यम् ॥ ९॥

Asadakaraṇādupādānagrahaṇātsarvasambhavābhāvāt |
śaktasyaśakyakaraṇātkāraṇabhāvāccasatkāryam ||9||

asat—something that does not exist
akaraṇāt—cannot produce anything
upādānagrahaṇāt—in all activities in the universe you are always able to find a material cause for
sarvasaṃbhavaabhāvāt—if you assume that nonexistence can create something, then anything can be created or imagined, but that is not the way this universe is. There is an order to the universe, things do not just happen—there is cause and effect—they happen in a particular way.
śaktasya śakyakaraṇāt—to produce something, there has to be a cause that has the capacity to produce
kāraṇabhāvāt ca satkāryam—ultimately the entire universe merges with mulaprakrti, hence the effects are also real

// Something that does not exist cannot produce something. Everything happens in a particular order, and only an entity or thing that has the capacity to do so can produce something. Since the entire universe merges with mulaprakriti, the effects are real. //

There is but one source; it produces different objects or effects that are similar, but there are also differences among them. In this sloka, Ishvarakrishna indicates some of the other views that prevailed in his day, which are reflected in some of the questions raised by my own students:

***Question*:** There is the view that you do not need to have a source for all things, that everything we experience is only our thoughts. Even though we see a number of objects, they can all be reduced to *cittavrittis*, thought processes. And if we eliminate the thoughts, what remains is nothing.
***Answer*:** If ultimately there is nothing, even those thoughts that you eliminated cannot have been produced in the first place. So, in everything we see there is always a material cause. For example, a pot is created by a potter, who is the intelligent or efficient cause (*nimittakarana*); the clay is the material cause (*upadanakarana*). In all the objects that we can perceive, the material cause consists of the five elements of earth, air, fire, water, and space. If we assume that nonexistence can create something, then anything can be created. But there is an order—things happen in a particular way. Only a thing that has the capacity to produce something can do so. And to produce something there has to be a cause that has the capacity to produce something. Hence the entire universe merges with mulaprakriti. You cannot merge with nothing. The universe is not an illusion, according to samkhyas and yogis. What is created is real (*sat*).

***Question*:** Mayavada, the doctrine that teaches that everything is an illusion, and Shunyavada, the view that consciousness lacks corresponding objects (also known as *shunya*)—are they the same?
***Answer*:** Before discussing Mayavada and Shunyavada, we must consider many well-known theories about the origin of the universe. According to Indian mythology and epics, the source of

the entire universe is the Worshipful Creator, the Bhagavan. He is both the material cause and the intelligent or efficient cause of this universe. So, the universe evolves from the Lord, is sustained by him, and ultimately merges into him.

In modern times the most well-known theory about the universe is the big bang theory. According to the big bang, the universe evolved out of a singularity, a unique plasma of extremely high-density matter at an incredibly high temperature and having enormous energy. According to some scientists, it is as small as a dime. It explodes with a bang and expands to the size of the universe, hence the "big bang." Ultimately, like the dissolution described by samkhyas and as is also found in Indian mythology, it all goes back into a big black hole of singularity.

Then we have a very detailed description of the evolution of the universe coming from samkhyas, which is totally endorsed by yogins. Accordingly, the source of the universe is the root substance, mulaprakriti. It is made of three characteristics, or gunas: sattva, rajas, and tamas. Order at the cosmic level is sattva, the energy for action in the universe or cosmic energy is rajas, and stability and inertia is tamas. Some scholars maintain that sattva is order, rajas is energy, and tamas is matter at the cosmic level. These three gunas are in equilibrium when in the mulaprakriti stage. The universe in turn evolves in stages from this root entity, the mulaprakriti. At the time of dissolution, they all merge back into the mulaprakriti, retracing the path of evolution in reverse.

Then we have the most revered philosophy in India, Vedanta. The word *Vedanta* means "acme of the Vedas." It is believed to be the ultimate teaching of the Vedas. There are many texts that explain this intricate philosophy. They are found in the Upanishads, which are texts that lead the aspirant step by step to an understanding of the ultimate reality. The Bhagavad Gita is also considered an important Vedanta text. This philosophy postulates that the ultimate reality is Brahman, which is unchanging, absolute consciousness. The word *Brahman* signifies an entity that grew into this huge universe. All creatures are subjects in a subject-object relationship in the world. The essential nature of the subject is consciousness or awareness of the objects, be they external objects or internal thoughts. This awareness, or what is also called the atman, is none other than Brahman, according to this theory. And with respect to the universe, the same Brahman is the source of the manifest universe. According to some Vedanta schools, the creation of the manifest universe from Brahman is real (*satkarya*). The Advaita or non-dual school of philosophy would say that the created universe is not real; it is an illusion. Objects that we experience in the world have three characteristics—a name, a form, and the substance. I am an entity in this world. I have a name, I have a form, and I am made of substances that weigh about 150 pounds or so. But according to the philosophy of illusion, Mayavada, the objects in the universe have only names and forms but no substance, and that is what the term *maya*, which loosely translates as "illusion," signifies. In fact, one of the Upanishads, a Vedanta text, says the universe is made of only names and forms (*namarupa*), which would amount to illusion. So in Vedanta the source is Brahman, but the effect, the universe, with its various objects, is real according to one school. But according to Advaita, it is not substantive, but an illusion. The great vedantin Gaudapada, the guru of the famous Advaita philosopher Adi Shankara's mentor Govinda Bhagavatpada, in the Mandukya Karika, asserts that no one is ever born and nothing is ever created.

Then we have Shunyavada, a philosophy that does not subscribe to the authority of the orthodox Vedic scriptures but has millions of followers nevertheless. According to this school of thought, the source of the universe is none of the above—not the singularity, not God, and not prakriti, Brahman, or whatever.

It's *shunya*, meaning an absence of anything. Shunya is the number 0 in Sanskrit and in several Indian languages. Patanjali, in his Yoga Sutras uses the term *shunya* a few times when he refers to *vastu shunya*, or the complete absence of an object. But then how can the manifest universe come from shunya? These philosophers concur with the mayavadins to aver that the manifest universe is only a projection and not an actual substantive creation. But how can we say that the universe that we are in and is real is an illusion? One has to meticulously follow their thought processes to see the weight of these philosophies. Here samkhyas say that the creation, its source, and the experiencing subject are all real.

***Question*:** Which came first? Buddhism or Vedanta?
***Answer*:** I don't know. Different scholars debate this. Buddhist ideas have been around for a very, very long time. In the Chandogya Upanishad, considered one of the oldest extant Vedic texts,* there is the statement *Sadeva somya idam agra aseet*—"Before this world was manifest, there was only existence, one without a second." What does this mean? In the beginning or before creation, only *sat*, Brahman, existed. This is mentioned in a conversation between a father and his son, who is seeking knowledge about the ultimate reality. The father tells his son that *sat* is existence, which is Brahman. Brahman alone existed in the beginning, and the universe evolved out of it. But in the Taittriya Upanishad, another major text dating from ancient times, it is said, *Asad va idam agram aseet*—meaning that initially there was *asat*, nonexistence, nothing existed. Some Shunyavada sects and other shunya philosophers point to this statement to claim that out of nothing came the universe.

*The Chandogya Upanishad is believed to have originated as early as the eighth century BCE.

Vedantins instead explain *asat* as unmanifested *sat*, or unmanifested Brahman. So all these competing philosophies existed more or less at the same time.

***Question*:** Does Yoga subscribe to the theory of *parinamavada*, that the cause is continually transforming into its effects?
***Answer*:** The word *parinamavada* is found in Vedanta. It is of two interpretations: *parinama vada* and *vivarta vada. Parinama vada* indicates that ultimately Brahman transforms itself into this visible universe. *Vivarta vada* says that Brahman, even as it does not undergo any change, appears to have created or changed into this universe. Here and for the yogi and samkhyas the phrase used is *satkaryavada*, "the effect is real." *Karya* means "effect."

***Question*:** You say *asat* means, basically, "nonexistence." Is this similar to purusha?
***Answer*:** No. *Asat* means something that does not exist. Purusha exists. *Asat* implies that there is nothing, that everything just came about. So, Samkhya does not accept that view. There has to be a cause, and we have to find the cause. You see an effect, whether the effect is an illusion or real, you have to find the cause. Even an illusion has to have a cause. Samkhyas say that mulaprakriti is the cause of the universe. Vedantins say the cause is not insentient prakriti, but the never-changing pure consciousness, or Brahman. Moreover, samkhyas say that the cause of the universe, which is mulaprakriti, is real, and the effect, the manifest universe, prakriti, also is real, so the creation is real. The Self, the subject that experiences the objects of the universe, is not the physical person, but the unvarying pure consciousness that is purusha or *jnah*. The purusha in all creatures is similar or identical—pure, unvarying consciousness—but it is not one and the same in all beings. Yogis such as Patanjali agree with samkhyas regarding the origin of the universe, the evolutionary stages, and the reality of the whole

process. They also agree with samkhyas with regard to the nature of purusha, the Self. Furthermore, they say that even as the universe is real, what each one experiences is a processed image of the outside world as a result of cittavrittis, that is, projections of the mind (*citta*). So Ishvarakrishna gives two proofs of the existence of mulaprakriti as the origin of the universe. First, nonexistence cannot produce anything. And second, ultimately the universe merges back into the cause, which is mulaprakriti.

Kārikā 10

The difference between cause and effect, between the unmanifest state of mulaprakriti and the manifest state of prakriti

हेतुमदनित्यमव्यापिसक्रियमनेकमाश्रितंलिङ्गम् ।
सावयवंपरतन्त्रंव्यक्तंविपरीतमव्यक्तम् ॥ १०॥

Hetumadanityamavyāpisakriyamanekamāśritaṃliṅgam |
sāvayavaṃparatantraṃvyaktaṃviparītamavyaktam ||10||

vyakta—the manifest, the evolutes
hetumat—has a cause
anityam—impermanent, changing
avyāpi—does not permeate, limited
sakriyam—all of them act, mulaprakriti does not act
āśritam—means all of them are supported by mulaprakriti and the three gunas
lingam—at dissolution, or during a mini-dissolution of cittavrittis in a yogi when everything merges into mulaprakriti

sāvayavam—there are many parts for each object
paratantram—they depend on something or are controlled by something else
avyaktam viparītam—unmanifest mulaprakriti is different from these

// The manifest universe has a cause. The universe is supported by mulaprakriti, unmanifest prakriti; the universe eventually merges back into mulaprakriti, but meanwhile it has many evolutes that are dependent on mulaprakriti, whereas the unmanifest universe is different from these. //

This sloka explains the important differences between manifest (*vyakta*) prakriti and the unmanifest mulaprakriti:

- The manifest universe, along with its beings and things (i.e., objects), has a prior cause (*hetumat*). Mulaprakriti, which is unmanifest prakriti, does not have a prior cause.
- All beings and things continually change (*anitya*); clay becomes a pot and so on. Mulaprakriti does not change; it has existed forever.
- Objects and beings do not pervade everywhere (*avyapi*); they take up a certain limited amount of time and space. The effects of mulaprakriti, which are the three qualities (*gunas*) of goodness and positivity (*sattva*), energy and activity (*rajas*), and limitations and restrictions (*tamas*), are ubiquitous and never-ending—the gunas permeate the whole universe.
- Manifest prakriti acts (*sakriyam*); unmanifest prakriti, which is mulaprakriti, does not act.
- The objects of manifest prakriti are many (*aneka*); mulaprakriti is singular.
- All objects in the manifest universe are supported by the unmanifest root essence that is mulaprakriti. They display

the three qualities (*gunas*) to varying degrees (*asrita*), yet this unmanifest prakriti does not depend on anything.

- At the time of dissolution, all manifest objects and entities merge into their previous cause and finally into the unmanifest mulaprakriti, the root substance, yet mulaprakriti has no cause in which to merge (*lingam*).
- Objects and entities consist of many parts (*savayava*); mulaprakriti has no parts.
- Whatever is manifest is controlled by something else (*paratantra*); mulaprakriti is independent.

Kārikā 11

The difference between prakriti and purusha; the distinction between the original root substance, mulaprakriti, and its evolutes on the one hand and the universal principle of purusha on the other; the difference between subject and object(s)

त्रिगुणमविवेकिविषयःसामान्यमचेतनंप्रसवधर्मि ।
व्यक्तंतथाप्रधानंतद्विपरीतस्तथा च पुमान् ॥ ११॥

Triguṇamavivekiviṣayaḥsāmānyamacetanaṃprasavadharmi |
vyaktaṃtathāpradhānaṃtadviparītastathā ca pumān ||11||

triguṇma—three gunas, namely *sattva*, *rajas*, and *tamas*
avivekī—nondiscriminating or lacking awareness or consciousness
viṣaya—objects
sāmānya—general, common
acetana—no consciousness

prasavadharmī—capable of evolving
vyakta—the manifest universe that consists of twenty-three of the twenty-five tattvas, or aspects of reality
tathā—likewise of three gunas
pradhāna—the principal one (synonym for *mulaprakriti*)
tadviparīta—entirely different from mulaprakriti and its evolutes
tathā ca—accordingly
pumān—soul, the conscious spirit

// Prakriti, both in its manifest and unmanifest forms, is comprised of the three qualities, or gunas—sattva, rajas, and tamas. Purusha, which is the Self, or consciousness, is entirely different. //

In the previous sloka, Ishvarakrishna brings out the differences between mulaprakriti, the root substance, and the various prakritic evolutes of mulaprakriti. In this sloka he explains that the entire material world has both its source and cause in mulaprakriti, and he asserts the critical difference between the manifest material world that is prakriti, and the unmanifest pure awareness that is purusha.

- The manifest universe and mulaprakriti (also called *pradhana*, "the chief cause of the material nature," as stated in the Shatapatha Brahmana) display the three gunas, or qualities—sattva, rajas, and tamas.
- Before the process of evolution begins, the three gunas are present in an unmanifest form, mulaprakriti, as a homogeneous, undifferentiated form (*aviveki*) in a state of equilibrium. For evolution to begin, this equilibrium needs to be disturbed by some cause in order to manifest its effect. In this way purusha and prakriti must come together.

- Reality is divided into subject and object. The manifest world is objective (*visayah*), that is, made of objects consisting of the five elements (*bhutas*). This manifest world and indeed the whole universe is an object of something else, while purusha, pure consciousness, is the subject that witnesses this creation and does nothing else but that.
- Prakriti, or the manifest universe, is common among all the subjects, that is, all the individual purushas.
- Mulaprakriti and the manifest universe that is prakriti do not have consciousness (*acetana*); purusha, on the other hand, is pure awareness (*cetana*).
- Though the manifest forms of prakriti lack consciousness, they can nevertheless reproduce other objects and forms, and by so doing they can evolve (*prasavadharmi*). This capability is unique to prakriti.

Purusha, the subject, as opposed to prakriti, the object, is neither sattvic, rajasic, or tamasic; it is pure consciousness, which neither mulaprakriti nor its twenty-three* (out of a total of twenty-five) tattvas possess. Purusha is entirely different from mulaprakriti and its manifest forms. What is common between mulaprakriti and the manifest universe (*vyakta*) is completely different from the nature of purusha.

***Question*:** So when you say "I am the subject," what then are the objects?
***Answer*:** We will come to that. That is why I need to define what the "I" really is. We have not gotten into this yet, but

*The presesnt discussion concerns the differences between mulaprakriti and its prakritic evolutes on one hand, and purusha on the other. The total number of tattvas (aspects of reality) is twenty-five, consisting of one purusha, one mulaprakriti, and twenty-three prakritic evolutes. So, the number of tattvas vary in this text depending on whether the discussion concerns only the manifest aspects of reality (i.e., prakriti) or all aspects of reality.

Ishvarakrishna explains it vividly later on in this text. Briefly, the way we go about life involves a subject-object relationship, so we have to define what the subject, the "I," is. Right at this moment we can see that there is an entity that is the subject and something else that is the object. Everything that is an object is prakriti according to the Samkhya Karika. This will be explained in the next few slokas.

***Question*:** How do you define consciousness?
***Answer*:** Consciousness is just awareness happening at the individual level. For example, at this moment there is an awareness of what's going on in my mind, an awareness of my thought processes, my cittavrittis. What goes on in my mind is whatever is presented by my senses to my mind, the resulting process occurring in my mind. And I am consciously aware of that. This is also explained in the Bhagavad Gita. The same consciousness experiences different thought processes as a child, as an adult, as an old person, and in the next lifetime. There is, however, only one awareness; it does not undergo any change, and it is aware of everything that goes on in my mind. Yesterday I may have been feeling out of sorts, while the previous day I was very happy. As a child, different thought processes were present, but the same purusha, the same consciousness or awareness, was experiencing those thoughts as is experiencing them now, without undergoing any change. There is an awareness in us that is different from whatever is going on in the mind as cittavrittis. I, the purusha as subject, is not sattvic, rajasic, or tamasic; this purusha does not undergo any change, whereas all the objects, which are the cittavrittis, keep on changing. It is a constant, unchanging awareness that observes everything that goes on in the mind. "I, Ramaswami, am happy in this particular moment, there is awareness of that." However, in the next moment I will experience something different, and so there will be an awareness of that. The "I" in both these instances is the subject. What is the essential nature of this subject? It is to be

aware of the object, and according to Patanjali the object is just the thought processes, or cittavrittis, at any given moment.

Question: Is there a difference between thoughts and awareness?
Answer: There's a difference, a big one, between thoughts and awareness. Awareness is purusha. It has none of the three gunas that characterize prakriti. Thought, cittavritti, is the object, and consciousness, purusha, is the subject.

Question: In mulaprakriti are the gunas in balance, in order?
Answer: Yes. And in prakritic objects they change and vary due to a countless number of possible permutations of the gunas. If mulaprakriti is a monolith or has only one characteristic, it cannot produce differences, it can only produce one thing, like a machine. But we have seen that because it too possesses the three gunas, it can produce innumerable varieties of objects. It is said that mulaprakriti is made of three strands, or three gunas, in a balanced but unmanifest state. The difference between mulaprakriti and its prakritic evolutes is that in the manifest state the gunas are in a state of imbalance—one of the three gunas will always dominate the other two. So, the differences in creation are inherent in mulaprakriti itself. In the next slokas, Ishvarakrishna explains how they operate in the manifest (*vyakta*) state.

The same consciousness that experiences everything during the waking state is the same consciousness that is able to experience what's going on in the dream state. When you are dreaming, you, the waking state you, are not experiencing the dream; your motor activities are completely paralyzed. When you lie down and go to sleep, the awareness of your own body goes away, and even if in a dream your dream self is running, your legs don't move, your arms don't move, and there is a temporary paralysis. The mind has completely identified with the dream self and not with the sleeping body. The next morning you may remember the dream, but when you're having the dream your mind has identified with your dream self and not with your body, the waking state person. And what is experiencing all of this? I, an eighty-five-year-old man, am not experiencing this. Whatever I consider myself to be during my dream is not the person my mind identifies myself to be during the waking state. So what is common between waking and dreaming? It is the awareness known as *purusha*. What if when you go to sleep you don't experience anything, nothing happens? In that case there is an experience of nothingness. And who experiences that peaceful state? That, again, is the awareness, the purusha.

Question: Where does purusha come from? Is its source mulaprakriti?

Answer: No, mulaprakriti refers to the root cause of various manifest forms or objects in a subject-object relationship. Where does consciousness, purusha, the subject, come from? From matter? No, matter is constantly changing. Consciousness does not undergo change. What does not change cannot come from what keeps on changing. Furthermore, there is a consciousness that is aware of everything that goes on all throughout one's lifetime. If I—my buddhi, i.e., my thinking faculty—can identify with that awareness as the true Self, then I will have attained the state of *kaivalya*, or freedom. Once you are convinced of that something which is unchanging, then whatever your state of mind may be in any given moment will not affect your purusha. Even though I see all kinds of objects around me or if I am sitting here and talking to you, all of this is happening in my mind. If I ask how I can see an object, what I see is an image created or processed in my mind. That is why Patanjali reduces all experiences to cittavrittis, thought processes. Cittavrittis are constantly changing—one moment thoughts are pleasant, then unpleasant, then boring, then stimulating, and so on. But nevertheless, there is an overarching awareness of every thought that takes place. That awareness is unchanging. Now I want my brain, my buddhi, to see the difference between the unchanging awareness of pure consciousness, purusha, and the changing cittavrittis. Patanjali says of this awareness, "*Sada jnatah citta vryttayah tat prabhoh purushasya aparinamitvat*," "All the cittavrittis are known all the time due to immutable nature of the purusha." The overarching awareness of everything that goes on in my mind from moment to moment is the true Self.

Question: How do you differentiate between memory and awareness?
Answer: Memory or remembering is one group of cittavrittis. Now you are listening to me, what is your cittavritti? You hear the sound produced by my speech and you try to bring something up that you have heard earlier in order to make sense of it. Then in the next moment you don't listen to me and have another cittavritti arising out of your memory. So that is why Patanjali classifies cittavrittis in five categories: *pramana*, or correct knowing at the moment; *viparyaya*, or incorrect knowing; *vikalpa*, fantasy or imagination; *smriti*, recollection or memory; and *nidra*, the voidness of deep sleep. So sometimes you don't listen to what's being said because you are engrossed in your own thoughts, recollecting from past information stored in the brain. The mind weaves many different thoughts; you, the real you, becomes aware of these thoughts, and the entity that is aware of the thoughts is your purusha, which is the true Self.

Kārikā 12

The characteristics of the three gunas that constitute prakriti and their way of operating

प्रीत्यप्रीतिविषादात्मकाः प्रकाशप्रवृत्तिनियमार्थाः ।
अन्योऽन्याभिभवाश्रयजननमिथुनवृत्तयश्चगुणाः ॥ १२॥

Prītyaprītiviṣādātmakāḥprakāśapravṛttiniyamārthāḥ |
anyo'nyābhibhavāśrayajananamithunavṛttayaścaguṇāḥ ||12||

prīti—desirable, uplifting, wholesome, kind, loving (what is sattvic)
aprīti—undesirable, duhkha (what is rajasic)
viśāda—stupefying, restraining (what is tamasic)
atmakaah—inherent qualities
prakāśa—clear, clarity
pravṛtti—activate, energy
niyama—restrain, matter
arthah—the purpose
anyonyaḥ —work together intimately
abhibhāva—one guna dominates at a time
āśraya—depends on one another
janana—produce an effect (the effect produced is based on all three)
mithuna—even though their characteristics are different they function together
vṛtti—activities of
guṇāḥ —the three gunas (sattva, rajas, and tamas)

// Desirable, undesirable, and stupefying or incapacitating are the inherent qualities of the three gunas, as are clarity, energy, and restraint the effects. The gunas are such that one guna dominates the other two at any given time (*abhibhava*); they work together (*anyonya*); they depend on one another (*asraya*); they produce an effect (*janana*); and though their characteristics differ, they operate in harmony with one another (*mithuna*). //

After explaining the difference between unmanifest mulaprakriti and manifest prakriti in the previous slokas, and establishing that these are to be distinguished from purusha, Ishvarakrishna goes into greater detail here on the nature of the three gunas that comprise prakriti and the fact of their interdependence—like three strands of a rope woven together.

The first attribute, *priti*, means desirable, uplifting, and wholesome and is associated with sattva. The aim of priti is to be exhibiting clarity, order, and illumination (*prakasa*).

The second attribute, *apriti*, means undesirable or uncomfortable and is associated with rajas; it implies the opposite of priti according to the rules of Sanskrit (the prefix a before a word indicates its opposite).

The next attribute, *visada*, means stupefying or restraining and is associated with tamas. The objective of tamas is to restrain (*niyama*); this brings grounding, restraint, and stability to the other two gunas.

There is order in the universe (sattva); there is energy to propel things into action (rajas); and there is stability (tamas) to balance the other two aspects of prakriti.

How do the gunas operate? They work closely together (*anyonya*) and are interdependent; one always dominates (*abhibhava*), while the other two work together to offer support.

This karika says that mulaprakriti is the source of the manifest universe, and that it is made of three intertwined strands that are the three gunas. This explains the various objects of the universe. Scientists say that the universe evolved out of a singularity, but it is difficult to understand how a monolithic singular plasma of high density and heat could produce the variegated universe. Vedantins talk about a unitary Brahman as both the material and efficient cause of the universe. At the same time, however, Advaita vedantins address the paradox of how such a wide variety of objects could come out of a homogeneous, singular Brahman by saying that the universe is unsubstantive and a mere illusion, like a dream. This approach is unique. It is customary to compare mulaprakriti to a rope or a twine made of three twisted strands of white, red, and black. Black represents tamas, red represents rajas, and white represents sattva. It is said that the gunas depend on one another or lean on one another (*asraya*); that an effect is produced by the combination of the three (*janana*); and there is no enmity among them—they work together intimately, as if they are one and the same (*mithuna*).

Though the gunas have different characteristics, they work in unison. For example, when we are sattvic, the energies of rajas and tamas do not interfere and we are able to think well, as rajas contributes the necessary energy. Tamas dominates when we go to sleep. If the strong energy of rajas comes at that time, we get nightmares, but sattva will support sweet dreams and peaceful sleep (*satvika nidra*).

Ishvarakrishna then proceeds to describe the specific activities of each guna and how each one is supported by the other two. *Vritti* means "activity." *Anyonya* implies mutuality. So, we have an intimate connection between the three gunas, but one always dominates (*abhibhava*). For example, when sattva dominates it controls rajas and tamas and produces a state of peace, clarity, and other sattvic qualities. Likewise, if rajas dominates, it will keep sattva and tamas in check and exhibit energy, anger, and other rajasic manifestations in the person. In a similar way, if tamas were to dominate, it would overpower sattva and rajas and exhibit its negative characteristic of stupidity or dullness.

The gunas depend on one another, as indicated by the term *asraya*. For example, sattva by itself alone cannot produce any activity (*vritti*) or any thoughts (*cittavrittis*). Supposing a person thinks deeply about an obscure or esoteric matter; sattva would then dominate at that time. But deep thinking needs energy. Depending on how much energy is needed, the thinking activity will require rajas. And the extent of rajas needed will depend on the influence of tamas, which would restrain. So, sattva can help the thinking function, rajas can provide the energy, and tamas can regulate the amount of energy needed for this activity and bring sleep and rest after long hours of intense concentration.

The gunas work together to change or produce something. This is represented by the Sanskrit term *janana*, "working together to create an effect." New things are produced by existing things and in the process all three gunas work together, but with one guna dominating the other two. At the time of creating something new, what is produced is perfect if sattva dominates, but imperfect if rajas dominates, and incomplete or defective if tamas dominates. In the Gita, the question of finding the nature of the Self is discussed. The Lord says that to consider the physical body as the individual Self is tamasic, that is, there is very little thought being given to the question. On the other hand, if a decision is arrived at after an incomplete evaluation or by drawing hasty conclusions (like the view that there are multiple atmans), then it is due to the dominance of rajas. The conclusion that there is one and only one consciousness as Vedanta maintains would be called a sattvic, or complete and thorough, evaluation.

It is also mentioned that the gunas work closely together (*mithuna*) and are inseparably entwined, like Siamese triplets. All three take part in all activities to varying degrees, but one of these qualities always dominates in a person. Some people are basically sattvic, some rajasic, and others tamasic, though the relatively dorment gunas will always come into play.

Kārikā 13

Continuation of the discussion of the qualities of the three gunas at an individual level and how they function in unison, like an oil lamp

सत्त्वंलघुप्रकाशकमिष्टमुपष्टम्भकंचलं च रजः ।
गुरुवरणकमेवतमःप्रदीपवच्चार्थतोवृत्तिः ॥ १३॥

Sattvaṃlaghuprakāśakamiṣṭamupaṣṭambhakaṃcalaṃ ca rajaḥ |
guru varaṇakamevatamaḥ pradīpavaccārthatovṛttiḥ ||13||

sattvam—sattvic quality
laghu—lightness of the body
parākāśkam—clarity of the mind
iṣṭam—desirable, consensus
upaṣṭamabhakam—activity
calam ca—inability to concentrate, instability
rahjah—rajas energy
guruḥ—heavy
varaṇakam—completely covered
tamaḥeva—is tamas indeed
pradīpavaccārthato—like a lamp with the constituents
vrittih—their activity

// Sattva manifests as lightness of the body and clarity of the mind, rajas as incessant physical activity and restlessness of the mind, and tamas as heaviness of the body and inertia of the mind. Like an oil lamp, all three gunas work in unison. //

In this sloka, Ishvarakrishna says the three gunas can be experienced or identified within ourselves as follows:

Sattva: At the physical level, sattva manifests as lightness of the body, while at the mental level there is clarity of the mind. Sattva is a desirable quality. Through the *yamas* (moral discipline) and *niyamas* (observances) of Yoga we try to reduce the rajasic and tamasic influences of the outside world so as to bring up sattva in the mind.

Rajas: At the physical level, rajas manifests as activity; on the mental level it is an inability to concentrate.

Tamas: At the physical level tamas produces heaviness; on the mental level, blankness and confusion.

Like an oil lamp,* the three gunas, the basic constituents of prakriti, work in unison. An oil lamp has three constituents: the flame that gives light is compared to sattva. The oil gives the necessary energy and is compared to rajas. The wick provides stability and is compared to tamas. Any two cannot do the job. A lamp requires all the three components. Any two won't do.

- Oil and wick: nothing happens.
- Wick and flame: the wick burns in no time.
- Oil and flame combined is uncontrolled wildfire.

Patanjali's Yoga Sutras say that since sattva is a desirable quality because it produces an agreeable mental space (*sukha*), one should make it the dominant quality. Can one just wish for sattva? Here the term *samskara* should be understood. According to Vedic philosophy, the mind, or citta, is a collection of habits, which are the samskaras: "*Samskara sesham hi cittam,*" or, "Samskaras are well-rooted habits that remain in the brain."

*The metaphor used here refers to an old-fashioned oil lamp that has a wick and a flame, a type of lamp still regularly used in Indian homes and temples. Oil lamps are revered in India and are a feature of shrines.

By and large, once a samskara is set, it is difficult to change; mere wishing is not sufficient. Samskaras are very powerful. People who are habitually sattvic will tend to remain sattvic all throughout life. But those who are habitually rajasic or tamasic will tend to have a disagreeable mental space or bad habits. In general, people tend to continue to operate in the same groove. An angry young person eventually becomes an angry old person, unless necessary steps are taken to change the deeply rooted habits or samskaras.

But unhelpful samskaras *can* be changed. And that change is brought about by yoga practice. In the initial stages, the practice of yoga turns a tamasic person into a rajasic person and then into a sattvic person. By following the yamas and nimayas, one can reduce the ingestion of rajas and tamas from the outside world. Patanjali says asana practice reduces the extremes of opposites (*dvandas*), such as success and failure, hot and cold, or other such opposites. For example, a rajasic person is completely elated when success comes and is completely depressed with the appearance of failure. A regular yoga practice will reduce rajas and thereby the practitioner will be less and less affected by the extremes of opposite pairs. In other words, less rajas means more equanimity. In a similar vein, pranayama, yogic breathing, helps reduce tamas so that sattva eventually can dominate.

Note that it is not enough to only practice yoga asanas to reduce rajas, because after stand-alone asana work one's mental space gets taken over by tamas rather than by sattva. That is what happens in modern yoga practice. After doing asanas the way aerobic exercises are done, as is common nowadays, you're hot and sweating, and consequently rajas is reduced, but as a consequence a lot of tamas in the form of metabolic waste accumulates. In yoga, tamas is reduced significantly through pranayama practice. That is one reason why both Raja yoga and

Hatha yoga insist on practicing asana and pranayama in tandem. So, after an hour or more of asana practice that includes 108 sun salutations (*surya namaskar*), you'll be sweating and tired, which is when tamas takes over. Which is why it's important to do a moderate amount of pranayama practice after a workout on the mat to remove the tamasic waste.

If we meditate with one-pointedness (*ekagrata*), that is sattvic activity. Rather than allowing oneself to be in a stupor, in a tamasic state, or be agitated, in a rajasic state, we prepare the body physiologically to be less and less rajasic and tamasic and more sattvic by strengthening sattva through one-pointed meditation.

In a tamasic state, the mind is inattentive and sleepy, and no meaningful thought is going on. In a rajasic state there are many thoughts, hundreds of thoughts, coming and going, one after another. In a sattvic meditative state we have but one thought as we bring the mind to the same object again and again. This method of one-pointed (*dharana*) contemplation (*dhyana*) is a means to self-knowledge and samadhi, and it has been developed so that over a period of time a new set of samskaras, yogic samskaras, emerge. The yogic samskaras arise out of the reduction of tamas and rajas and the dominance of sattva. When the rajas and tamas are reduced through the practice of asana and pranayama, the mental space (*citta akasa*) vacated by these two gunas will be taken over by sattva, the most desirable quality or guna helpful for the higher pursuits of yoga. So the practice of yoga is a method by which our samskaras can be modified for the better. If I want to remove duhkha and understand the nature of the universe and the Self, that is possible only if sattva dominates, not rajas or tamas. Hence what Samkhya proposes, yoga accomplishes.

Kārikā 14

The inherent characteristics of a cause are seen in its effects; they have the same nature.

अविवेक्यादिहिसिद्धंत्रैगुण्यात् तद्विपर्ययाऽभावात् ।
कारणगुणात्मकत्वात्कार्यस्याव्यक्तमपिसिद्धम् ॥ १४॥

Avivekyādi hi siddhaṃtraiguṇyāttadviparyayābhāvāt |
kāraṇaguṇātmakatvātkāryasyāvyaktamapisiddham ||14||

avivekkyādi—absence of consciousness and the other characteristics
hi siddham—is determined
triguṇyāt—due to the three gunas
tadviparyaya—of the opposite
abhāvāt—not existing
kāraṇaguṇātmakatvāt—the three gunas of the cause are present
kāryasya—in the effects of the various tattvas
avyaktamapi—the unmanifest also
siddham—proved

// Both the effect, which is prakriti or the various evolutes, and the cause of that effect, mulaprakriti, have the same nature, just as an entity that has evolved from its parent entity has something in common with it—they are both made up of the same three gunas. *Aviveka*, referring to actions that lack an underlying consciousness, is a common characteristic among the three gunas. The effects of the gunas are palpable in the prakritic evolutes. Ultimately everything merges into

mulaprakriti, the source, which is comprised of the three gunas in unmanifest forms and in a state of equilibrium. //

Both the unmanifest mulaprakriti and the manifest world of prakriti consist of the three gunas, just as an entity that has evolved from its parent entity shares a common nature with the parent. Because the three gunas permeate the universe, this is proof that mulaprakriti, the unmanifest root source, also possesses the three gunas, but in an unmanifest state. We are able to experience these three gunas in mulaprakriti's various evolutes, therefore we must infer that mulaprakriti also possesses the three gunas.

Kārikā 15

Five reasons that prove the existence of mulaprakriti

भेदानांपरिमाणात्समन्वयाच्छक्तितःप्रवृत्तेश्च ।
कारणकार्यविभागादविभागाद् वैश्वरूपस्य ॥१५॥

Bhedānāṃparimāṇātsamanvayācchaktitaḥpravṛtteśca |
kāraṇakāryavibhāgādavibhāgādvaiśvarūpasya ||15||

bhedānāṃ—different things, objects, people
parimāṇāt—are finite, limited
samanvayat—even if they are finite, there is something they have in common, namely, the three gunas
shaktitah pravrteh—objects get the gunas from the source
karana karya vibhagat—since there is a difference between cause and effect

karana—instrument of action
karya—action
vibhagat—separation
vaisvarupasya avibhagat—even though all these objects are different, ultimately, they are going to merge with the mulaprakriti.

// The nature of mulaprakriti, even though it cannot be seen, can be known from the nature of its effects, which can be perceived as the manifested form of the objects of the universe. There are five reasons why mulaprakriti exists: *bhedanamparinamat*, *samanvaya*, *saktithpravrttesca*, *karanakaryavibhagat*, and *vaisvarupasya*. //

In this continuation of the previous sloka, Ishvarakrishna asserts that in all the different things of the universe, even though all these objects are limited and finite, we can perceive what they all have in common: the three gunas.

There is a difference between the cause, mulaprakriti, and the effect, prakriti. But despite their difference, all the prakritic evolutes will ultimately merge with mulaprakriti in the final dissolution.* So, we have to infer that mulaprakriti exists.

There are five proofs for the existence of mulaprakriti:

1. The five elements combine to create many objects, which are finite, limited, and measured (*bhedanamparinamat*).

2. Even though they are finite, there is something common to all of them, and that is the three gunas; the balance of the gunas may vary, but all three nevertheless permeate the entire universe (*samanvayat*).

---

*Here, the final dissolution refers to both the microcosm, i.e., the individual when he or she attains kaivalya when the gunas attain *samyavasta* or equilibrium, as well as the macrocosm that is the entire universe merging with mulaprakriti at the time of *pralaya*.

3. The potential to create exists within the mulaprakriti (*saktithpravrittesca*).

4. There is a difference between the cause, which is mulaprakriti, and the different evolutes (*karanakaryavibhagat*).

5. Ultimately the universe merges into the all-pervading mulaprakriti (*vaisvarupasya*), the cosmic root substance.

The imprints of the gunas are palpable in every aspect of the universe. At the cosmic level there is matter and energy, huge quantities of both, and they are attributable to rajas and tamas. Then what of sattva? Sattva is order, cosmic order or universal order. There is order in every aspect of the universe—an electron, a cell, or the Milky Way, all function according to inherent order. In individual creatures there is order (*dharma*) and peace (*shanti* or *sukha*) due to sattva. Then due to rajas there is energy—biological, emotional, and intellectual. There is restraint, matter, and chaos due to tamas. So according to Samkhya the three gunas are palpable in every evolute of the universe. It is in the imbalance or varied proportions among the three gunas that we find a variety of objects, feelings, and so forth.

Kārikā 16

The innumerable objects in the universe are brought about by the intermingling of the three gunas, which in turn prove the existence of the mulaprakriti as the cause behind all manifestations.

कारणमस्त्यव्यक्तंप्रवर्ततेत्रिगुणतःसमुदयाच्च ।
परिणामतःसलिलवत्प्रतिप्रतिगुणाश्रयविशेषात् ॥ १६॥

Kāraṇamastyavyaktaṃpravartatetriguṇataḥsamudayācca |
pariṇāmataḥsalilavatpratipratiguṇāśrayaviśeṣāt ||16||

avyaktam—unmanifested (mulaprakriti)
karanam—cause, instrument of action
asti—exists
trigunatah—means, it is made up of three gunas
samudayaat—three gunas permeate the entire universe
salilavat—like water
prati-prati—individual, every object
gunaashraya—residing in the gunas, support of one guna to the other
visheshaat—of uniqueness of every object
parinamatah—modified

// The unmanifest (*avyakta*, or mulaprakriti) is comprised of the three gunas, which permeate the entire manifest universe, like rainwater falling on different soils; this results in myriad unique combinations, all of which testify as to their cause, mulaprakriti. //

In mahat tattva, or the cosmic intelligence principle, sattva dominates, but the other two gunas are also present to allow it to function in a particular way. In the ahamkara tattva, or the cosmic energy principle, rajas dominates, but the other gunas are also there. The group of five tanmatras are tamasic evolution supported by other gunas. All three gunas permeate the entire universe, although objects appear to be different. Because of the uniqueness of each object, it could be inferred that in some objects sattva dominates, while in others rajas or tamas, and even then the proportions vary. In some people or objects sattva dominance could be very high or of different degrees. So, it is also the case for the dominance of rajas and tamas. Every object supports the gunas differently.

Kārikā 17

Establishing the existence of purusha as distinct from mulaprakriti and the creative principle

सङ्घातपरार्थत्वात्त्रिगुणादिविपर्ययादधिष्ठानात् ।
पुरुषोऽस्तिभोक्तृभावात् कैवल्यार्थं प्रवृत्तेश्च ॥ १७॥

Saṅghātaparārthatvāttriguṇādiviparyayādadhiṣṭhānāt |
puruṣo'stibhoktṛbhāvātkaivalyārthaṃpravṛtteśca ||17||

sanghata—collection, assemblage of an object
pararthatvat—for someone to enjoy, for another entity, a subject
trigunadiviparyayat—and that entity is different from the three gunas, as they keep changing
adhisthanat—unchanging
bhoktrabhavat ca—there has to be an experiencer for experiences
kaivalyartham—to be able to achieve the ultimate goal of freedom from samsara
pravritteh—prakriti acts

// Because there is an experience taking place, there has to be an experiencer. This is the purusha, which does not possess the three gunas. Prakriti, which does, gives different experiences to the unchanging awareness or supreme consciousness that is the purusha and thereby helps us achieve ultimate liberation, or kaivalya. //

The objects of the universe belong to the prakriti, but for the sake of purusha, pure consciousness, they act, because it is in the nature of prakriti to provide experiences—good sometimes, but mostly painful—to the purusha, to merely witness. And this same prakriti can thereby lead to eternal freedom for the person.

Because experiences take place in us in the mind, or citta, and arise as thoughts, or cittavrittis, there has to be an experiencer. Some of everything that happens in this universe has to be experienced by some consciousness or awareness that exists beyond the physical entity. There has to be a consciousness that is unchanging. That entity is entirely different from the three gunas, which constantly change.

This body as well as the entire universe of objects is collected for the benefit of the true Self so as to be able to experience happiness and achieve ultimate kaivalya and freedom from the prakritic experiences of samsara. There has to be and there is a purusha, a Self beyond the three gunas that witnesses.

To attain freedom, you don't have to go anywhere; you can use your body-mind complex, and instead of spending time doing lots of mundane things, spend time trying to understand the nature of the Self. Contemplate and do yoga practice, the whole range of practices, not just asana. The mind can give experiences and also reach a state of *citta vritti nirodha*, a cessation of the myriad activities of the mind that provides a permanent, painless, sorrowless state. As the Yoga Sutras (4.18) say,

Sada jnatah cittavryttayah tat prabhoh purushasya aparinamitvat.

The various cittavrittis, be they truth or untruth, imagination, sleep, or remembering, are always experienced because of the nonvarying, constant awareness, the purusha.

This sutra confirms the existence of purusha by establishing the independent existence of the Self. The constantly changing cittavrittis are known and can be experienced by this unchanging consciousness, this purusha. What is going on in my mind all the time is known to me, the real me, the subject, the Self. Patanjali, in the Yoga Sutras (2.18), says,

Prakash kriya sthithishilam bhutendriyatmakam bhogapavargartam drishyam

The seen (objective world) is of the nature of clarity, activity, and inertia, the three gunas. It consists of the subtle and gross elements and sense organs (indriyas—five senses of action and five senses of perception). Its purpose is to experience a release (of the Self).

The manifest, often erroneously considered the true Self by most people, is made of *prakasa*, or clarity, which is sattva; *kriya*, or activity, which is rajas; and *sthiti*, or restraint, which is tamas. These three gunas or universal chracterestics exist in varying proportions. The manifest is also made up of a combination of the five *bhutas*, or gross elements: earth (solid matter), water (liquid matter), energy (fire matter), air (gaseous matter), and space. As well it consists of five subtle elements, or *tanmatras*: touch, sound, light/form, taste, and smell. Then it has the ten *indriyas*, or sense organs—five of action and five senses of perception. Add to it the three *anthkaranas*, or internal organs, which are manas (the mind), buddhi (the intellect), and ahamkara (the ego). These thirteen—the ten indriyas plus the three anthkaranas—constitute indriyas in this sloka. How can this nonself be considered to be the Self? This physical body-mind complex exists in order to have varied experiences that are incessantly presented to the Self. The yogi uses this nonself or the the prakritic body-mind complex to achieve kaivalya, or final, irreversible freedom—freedom from the three types of duhkha.

Here *drishyam*, or "what is seen," refers to the pseudoself. This person, this body, this mind is commonly yet erroneously seen as the true Self. It consists of the three gunas. This body (*drishya atma*, the body that can be seen and experienced) can be used for experiencing happiness in physical form or to attain permanent freedom (*apavarga*) from three types of endless duhkha—the suffering of suffering, the suffering of change, and the all-pervasive suffering that colors life in general.

It is the answer to the question as to what one should do with one's life, to wit: I can use my life for endless experiences, which are mostly painful, or I can follow yogic discipline based on Samkhya philosophy and attain the permanent freedom called kaivalya by yogis and samkhyas.

Sanghata, "assemblage," is the word used in Samkhya to describe the physical self consisting of prakritic parts. Patanjali uses the words *drishya* or *drishyaatma*, implying that which can be seen and experienced, to describe this false self. Both philosophies say it all depends on the individual as to how to use this empirical person during one's lifetime. It can be used more and more for worldly experiences, which will yield nothing more than the three types of endless duhkha; or by following Samkhya philosophy and practicing yoga we can achieve lasting freedom. The choice is ours.

Here is a useful metaphor: Think of a bed as a *sanghata*, an assemblage of prakritic objects. It consists of four legs, a frame, a mattress, some sheets, two or more pillows, and maybe a blanket. All this is made for the sake of a person, the one who sleeps in the bed, who represents the purusha. The one who sleeps is the *para*, the subject mentioned in this sloka, and the assemblage is the bed made of different parts, representing the prakriti. So, the *sanghata*, that is, the bed, which represents the prakriti, is assembled for the benefit of the person who sleeps there, who represents the purusha.

Kārikā 18

Multiple consciousnesses, each with an individual purpose, exist within each person.

जनन१मरणकरणानां प्रतिनियमादयुगपत्प्रवृत्तेश्च ।
पुरुषबहुत्वंसिद्धं त्रैगुण्य२विपर्ययाच्चैव ॥ १८॥

Jananamaraṇakaraṇānāṃpratiniyamādayugapatpravṛtteśca |
puruṣabahutvaṃsiddhaṃtraiguṇyaviparyayāccaiva ||18||

janma, janana—birth
marana—death
karanam—activities, limbs, the body
pratiniyamat—for each and every individual, it is separate and differently defined
ayugapat pravrittesca—there is no connection between the span of life, death, bodies, and activities of one person and another
traigunya viparyat—the gunas vary from person to person; one is predominantly either sattvic, tamasic, or rajasic
purusa bahutvam siddam—a single purusha cannot experience all these permutations, so each individual has a separate purusha, making for a plurality of purushas

// **If there was only one universal consciousness, all beings would be born and would die at the same time. Our life, death, and activities are, however, different. The balance of the gunas in each person also varies. Because of this, there has to be a different purusha in each person.** //

We are born at different times, we die at different times, and we have different activities in our lives. Each and every person is differently defined. We are each unique, even as we share the same world with others. The balance of the gunas also varies in each person. One can therefore conclude that one purusha, one consciousness, cannot experience all these things at once in all beings. Each individual has a purusha that is unique and different from any other purusha. This makes for multiple purushas. And even though all the purushas are identical in terms of being pure consciousness, they are different and distinct in each person. This view departs from the single-purusha view of Vedanta.

***Question*:** Are the different purushas made of different samskaras?

***Answer*:** We are talking about the purusha, which is different from the mind, or citta, which is prakriti. Samskaras pertain to prakriti, not to purusha. In this sloka, Ishvarakrishna argues against the Vedantic or Upanishadic view that there is only one single purusha, one consciousness (*paramapurusha*). He refutes this idea by pointing out that there are variations across life, death, activities, bodies, and the balance of the gunas in each person. Vedanta says that these variations pertain to prakriti and not to purusha. They maintain that there is only one purusha or Brahman, and in each person the mind reflects that one consciousness. But Ishvarakrishna disagrees, saying that each entity has a unique lifetime and experiences unique to that being, so there must be a uniquely individual purusha in each person. There is a different span of life and there is a different experience for each life span, and so there has to be different purushas, different consciousnesses.

All of you in front of me have an individual consciousness, a separate purusha from everyone else's, according to both the Samkhya and Yoga philosophies. From my experience, all the people in front of me are part of my cittavrittis, my thoughts, and my body is also part of my thoughts, and this entire being of mine—my body, my thoughts, and my experience of the people in front of me—is being witnessed by one purusha, one consciousness: my own individual purusha.

Mayavada is a doctrine that rejects all forms and manifestations and says that everything is an illusion, everything is ultimately one consciousness, and the goal is to merge with that oneness—a doctrine that vedantists subscribe to. What then is the point in saying that each of the objects or entities I experience in this illusion have a separate consciousnesses? If the entire universe is an illusion as Mayavada asserts, then there is no point in saying that each being has a separate purusha. Let's say I have a dream, which is an illusion, in which I am chased by a tiger, and a number of friends are laughing at me. My dream self had a bad experience that was witnessed by whom? Is there a consciousness in the dream fellow that experiences it? No, say those who subscribe to Mayavada doctrine. It is just an illusion. The dream entity did not have real legs, has no brain, and yet appears to think and run. So, if I were to agree with vedantins that the entire world is an illusion, then to ask if each person in the illusion has a consciousness would be an irrelevant question, they would argue.

Samkhya differs from Vedanta in this regard. Samkhyas say there is a unique consciousness in each and every person because each one of us is real, and the universe we are in is real and substantive. This philosophy maintains that there is an unchanging consciousness that experiences all that goes on in the mind as cittavrittis, thoughts. Even though we experience the entire universe outside of us, everything gets reduced to a cittavritti before an experience can take place. How do I see you, my friend? The light falls on you, the sense of sight comes to me, the signals are sent to my brain, and the result is projected as a cittavritti. I perceive not only this cittavritti, but everything outside of me, as well as the physical me. I also feel that I, the individual prakriti, is sitting and talking to all of you. Cittavritti is a totality of the entire experience—of me talking, you sitting there listening, and so forth at a given moment. So, the cittavritti has to include whatever I consider to be me, along with something else that is witnessing this cittavritti, and that is my purusha.

***Question*:** What if the purusha is in so many ways the opposite of prakriti? How can all purushas be the same?

***Answer*:** Essentially all purushas are identical but they are not the same. Let's say you and I each have a five-rupee note. They are identical in value, they are exactly the same form, but they are not the same piece of paper. Likewise, the purushas in you and me are identical but not the same. In contrast, vedantins say there is only one purusha watching an illusory world.

***Question*:** So the purusha does not have a life span?
***Answer*:** Something that does not change has no beginning or end. As samkhyas and yogins we must identify with the unchanging purusha that is the true Self, the subject. But how do we do that? We may say, "Oh, I'm getting older, I've got all kinds of aches and pains." I may see myself as an old man with a perishable body-mind. But this old man has a consciousness that has not aged and will never age. If my mind, my buddhi, is able to contemplate that and identify with that as the true Self, I can then realize my immortality. That's the main message here. If you are immortal, why worry about the inevitable death? You don't have to take my word for this. Sit down, contemplate, and come to the conclusion that this body is not the true Self. Yet thinking of the body as the true Self is a fundamental misconception we humans have. Samkhyas dispel this misunderstanding by saying that there is a purusha that is unchanging and eternal. It is neither produced nor does it produce anything, and it does not change. It cannot die since it does not undergo any changes. The main message of all this is that we worry about the body, which, being prakriti, is not our true Self; instead, we (via our buddhi, the thinking faculty) must recognize the purusha as the consciousness that witnesses everything that is prakriti, including the body.

***Question*:** Then is there no samadhi like there is in yoga?
***Answer*:** When one stills the mind in order to experience the ultimate reality (*citta vritti nirodha*), this brings freedom. When the

individual mind realizes the true nature of the Self as unchanging and immortal, pure consciousness, the mind will be happy and satisfied. If someone comes and says there is something else that will make you happy, it says, "No, I know the true nature of myself and there is no further interest in my mind to get engaged in all these activities." There is finally no more discursive thoughts, and cittavrittis cease. At this point don't worry about others. The only way you can help another person is to educate her or him in the way you helped yourself. When I know the true Self, I know who I really am. And then the mind will stop.

Question: In the Yoga Sutras, the frame of reference is the individual, so in Samkya is the frame of reference the universe?
Answer: No, even in Yoga the reference to the universe is there. However, Yoga doesn't go into as much detail on this subject as Samkhya, which says that for the mind to come to the complete satisfied state it has to understand the nature of the universe, the prakritic evolution, and the individual subject, the Self. However, Yoga does give a framework for achieving liberation. From the myriad cittavrittis that happen in ordinary humans, the practice of yoga can substantially reduce these discursive thoughts by reducing the cittavrittis to single vritti during meditation, then entering a state of samadhi, and further deepening in and culminating in the state of *nirodha*, in which all thoughts cease. So, the Yoga Sutras are aimed at liberation.

Samkhya's goal is the same as Yoga's. Samkhya first explains evolution, and then the path of freedom from all suffering. According to Samkhya, with a complete understanding of the Self, the nature of the universe, and the nature of evolution, the mind will come to a stop. With this knowledge, yogis may say, "Now we understand what is to be known." But even though we have understood and contemplated and are convinced about it, because our old samskaras about what constitutes the true Self are not sufficiently weakened and new ones have not yet arisen as samskaras, the mind is likely to drift away and fall back into the old habit of considering the body-mind complex as the Self. So, I need to be able to see it directly. I need a new discipline, a new set of samskaras. In Samkhya we get indirect knowledge (*parokshajnanam*) of the Self through the senses or through the intellect. We can then contemplate the nature of the Self, infer its existence, and become convinced of it. This then leads to, or may lead to a direct experience of the Self. According to Samkhya, this process is achieved through a set of mental modes that eventually reduce to a single thought (*pratyaya*), and then dissolution of all thoughts—but this process may not be possible for everyone. That is where Yoga comes in to make this quest possible for anyone interested in avoiding future pain, through the practice of Kriya yoga, Ashtanga yoga, and Samadhi yoga.

Question: What is the difference between samadhi and liberation, kaivalya?
Answer: The Yoga Sutras say that samadhi is one characteristic state or capability of the mind. It is total concentration, where you (that is, your brain, your buddhi) forget about your physical self and can contemplate the twenty-four prakritc tattvas so that ultimately you know the difference between the mind and its thoughts, and you can stay in that state. In samadhi you can focus on any of the different aspects of reality. Ultimately when you (i.e., your sattvic buddhi) are able to contemplate the nature of the true Self—which is the purusha, the twenty-fifth tattva—the mind will stop thinking, as there is nothing left to contemplate. This is called *nirodhah samadhi*, the cessation of thoughts. There is also *samprajnata samadhi*, in which the yogi is able to experience direct knowledge of the prakritic tattvas. So samadhi is of different types; in all, the witnessing activity of the consciousness is the same, but what you contemplate and what results come out of it is what defines the nature of your samadhi. There is *nirvikalpa samadhi*, a meditative state of total

absorption achieved by advanced meditator; *nirodha samadhi*, the cessation of all thoughts; and *nirbija samadhi*, a object-less samadhi in a state of kaivalya or total freedom.

Okay, now let's consider kaivalya, liberation. When the mind recognizes the true Self, the purusha is free. What happens then is that the purusha is no longer required to watch all the nonsense that goes on in the mind as thoughts. Everything comes to a stop and all is peaceful. The purusha knows everything. In our ordinary experience the mind never stops churning out thoughts, but yogis and the samkhyas recognize that there is a stage when the mind can and will come to a stop. When will the mind come to a stop? When the mind knows what is to be known, it finally settles down. Suppose you are very anxious, sitting at home, because someone dear to you has gone abroad and you are waiting to hear that the person has reached their destination. Until you get the news, you are anxious, restless. The moment you get the call, there is relief. Likewise, when you (your buddhi or intelligence principle) realize what the true Self is, you cannot be affected by anything that happens in the prakriti. This leads to an absolute state of inner peace. This cannot happen by merely reading or listening to somebody. You have to sit and experience it directly, and that is where yoga practice can help.

Kārikā 19

The distinct characteristics of purusha

तस्माच्च विपर्यासात्१ सिद्धंसाक्षित्वमस्यपुरुषस्य ।
कैवल्यंमाध्यस्थ्यंद्रष्टृत्वमकर्तृभावश्च ॥ १९॥

Tasmāccaviparyāsātsiddhaṃsākṣitvamasyapuruṣasya |
kaivalyaṃmādhyasthyaṃdraṣṭṛtvamakartṛbhāvaśca ||19||

tasmat—from that
viparyasat—being entirely different
asya purushasya—this purusha or consciousness is
sakshi tvam—mere observance
siddham—it is proved, can be proved
tata—further
kaivalya—single, isolated, detached, liberation
maadhyastam—is not disturbed by whatever is happening in the mind, neutral
drshtutvam—keeps on observing
akartru tbhavasca—does not do anything whether you are miserable or happy

// In contrast to prakriti, purusha lacks the three gunas, hence it cannot perform any actions on its own; its nature is to be a witness to the drama of prakriti. The purusha does not undergo any change; it maintains neutrality, it does not do anything, it merely observes. //

That all of our experiences are only cittavrittis is one of the biggest contributions of Yoga philosophy. Even though there are a multitude of activities, they are all reduced to cittavrittis. These then are divided into five groups. In contrast, the only thought or *vritti* that Samkhya considers is *pramana vritti*, correct knowing—I want to know the truth about the Self and everything else about the objective universe.

Patanjali says that ordinarily everyone has not only *pramana vritti*, they also have *vikalpa*, fantasy or imagination; *viparyaya*, incorrect knowing; *nidra*, deep sleep; and *smriti vritti*, memory. He puts all this together and frames a different viewpoint: to reduce cittavrittis, one must drastically reduce the clutter of these categories of thought so that the mind will be able to understand the true nature of the Self and come to a complete standstill. *Citta vritti nirodha* is therefore the most important message of Yoga, and the three gunas is a concept shared by both Samkhya and Yoga.

Kārikā 20

On the difficulty of distinguishing between purusha and the mind, or buddhi

तस्मात्तत्संयोगादचेतनंचेतनावदिवलिङ्गम् ।
गुणकर्तृत्वे च तथाकर्तेवभवत्युदासीनः ॥ २०॥

Tasmāttatsaṃyogādacetanaṃcetanāvadivaliṅgam |
guṇakartṛtve ca tathākartevabhavatyudāsīnaḥ ||20||

tasmat—since consciousness and activity are entirely different from each other

tat samyogat—because of the apparent coming together of linga or the buddhi with purusha

achetana—the entity which does not have consciousness

lingam—the mind, or buddhi, is an effect or product of the mulaprakriti, unmanifest form, into which it eventually merges

cetana—consciousness, purusha

iva—as if

guna—referring to the three gunas or the prakriti

gunakartrutve—the three gunas or prakriti alone act in unison

tatha—likewise, similarly

udasinah—the uninvolved purusha, the impersonal
bhavati—becomes
karta iva—as if the actor

// The body and mind are erroneously seen as the Self. Prakriti is only a blind doer and does not know. But sometimes it looks like purusha is doing an action. How is this so? Purusha doesn't do anything, it just observes. The experience of doing something, being conscious of an action, can only be had by the purusha. //

This sloka points out two common mistakes. Purusha, or consciousness, which is essentially a witness, *appears* to act. On the other hand, the mind, or buddhi, which has no consciousness, appears to have awareness. In fact, Vedic scholars have interpreted the word *citta* as "one who masquerades as consciousness" (*cit iva bhavayati iti cittam*). Vedantins call this *adhyasa* or *aropa*, meaning a false superimposition of an alien quality or characteristic. Considering the prakritic body-mind complex as having consciousness is a misconception; it is to superimpose pure consciousness, purusha, on prakriti. Moreover, considering purusha, pure consciousness, to have a physical, prakritic body-mind that acts is to superimpose the prakritic body on consciousness. This double mistake, say yogis and vedantins, is an incorrect understanding.

Because of the proximity of purusha and prakriti, it is very difficult to separate them, and hence it can look like prakriti has consciousness and purusha acts. This means that prakriti, which is not conscious and possesses the three gunas (while purusha does not possess the gunas), appears to be conscious, whereas in reality it is not. The sun, when reflected in water, will take on the qualities of the water, be it still and clear, rippling, or cloudy. It is not the sun that is moving or cloudy—the sun remains constant; it is only the water that changes.

This body-mind complex is made of the twenty-four prakritic tattvas (see page 29 in Kārikā 3 for the complete list of the twenty-five tattvas). It has no awareness and ultimately dissolves into the mulaprakriti. But it *appears* to have consciousness when thinking, acting, and so forth. Conversely, purusha, pure consciousness, *appears* to be doing all the activity because of its proximity to the prakritic body-mind complex, but its main task is to merely witness. The reality is that prakriti acts, and purusha witnesses.

***Question*:** I know the teachings say there is a difference between the mind and the witnessing Self, the purusha, however, I cannot seem to be able to understand the difference between these two.
***Answer*:** Let's consider the example of water and salt. When salt is added to water and thoroughly mixed, you will not be able to see the salt. But when you taste it, you know that it is not plain water. Likewise, ordinarily we (the buddhi intellect) do not see consciousness, the atman, and the physical body-mind complex as essentially different. But study and analysis would prove that they are distinctly different. Can we separate water and salt? Yes, by a process in which you heat the solution and the water evaporates, leaving behind the salt residue. You can then condense the steam and bring it back to its earlier state. Likewise, while practicing yoga in a state of samadhi, one can let one's buddhi experience the difference between the purusha and the prakritic body-mind complex (*prakriti-purusha viveka*).

Kārikā 21

The twin effects of the proximity of purusha and prakriti

पुरुषस्यदर्शनार्थं कैवल्यार्थं१ तथाप्रधानस्य ।
पङ्गवन्धवदुभयोरपिसंयोगस्तत्कृतःसर्गः ॥ २१॥

Puruṣasyadarśanārthaṃkaivalyārthaṃtathāpradhānasya |
paṅgvandhavadubhayorapisaṃyogastatkṛtaḥsargaḥ ||21||

purushasya—of the purusha
kaivalyartham—for the sake of its freedom
tatha—in the same way
pradhanasya—mulaprakriti means three gunas
darshanartam—to show the nature of the three gunas and understand the nature of mulaprakriti
panguandhavat—of a lame person and a blind person
tat kritah—the whole creation starts with the union of purusha and prakriti
sarga—evolution takes place by the togetherness of these two

// The purpose of life, according to Samkhya and Yoga, is to realize purusha and know the nature of prakriti. The reason why it is not ordinarily achieved is due to the proximity of purusha and prakriti (*samyoga*). Purusha does not do anything, but it is aware of everything that goes on in the prakritic mind (*citta*). //

Like a lame person and a blind person, purusha and prakriti come together. If they both want to achieve something that they cannot do individually, the lame person and the blind person have to come together. The lame person can see but cannot move; the blind person cannot see but can move. The lame person sits on the shoulders of the blind person and guides him. If the lame person sitting on the shoulders of the blind one does not know the way, the pair will be going in circles, never getting out of the forest. This is like what we all do all our lives, lifetime after lifetime. But when the lame person knows the way out of the deep, dark forest, both can reach their destination beyond the forest. At that point they no longer need each other, mission accomplished! Each becomes free, not tied to the other. Here

Ishvarakrishna uses the metaphor of the blind person and the lame person to illustrate the point that when two entities with different capabilities are unable to accomplish a task individually, they can join together to achieve their goal. Of course, this is a common experience in the world.

The whole of creation starts with the coming together (*samyoga*) of purusha and prakriti. The nonacting purusha and the acting prakriti come together and experiences take place. The goal of this union is ultimately, according to Samkhya, to free purusha and know the nature of the universe.

Kārikā 22

The process of universal evolution

प्रकृतेर्महांस्ततोऽहङ्कारस्तस्माद्गणश्चषोडशकः ।
तस्मादपिषोडशकात्पञ्चभ्यःपञ्चभूतानि ॥ २२॥

Prakṛtermahāṃstato'haṅkārastasmādgaṇaścaṣoḍaśakaḥ |
tasmādapiṣoḍaśakātpañcabhyaḥpañcabhūtāni ||22||

prakrteh—from the mulaprakriti (or *pradhana*)
mahan—evolves the greatest tattva or evolute
mahattattva—the greatest tattva, referring to the universal cosmic intelligence. Mahattattva is universal intelligence and the first evolute of prakriti. When the mahat is in a sattvic mode, it creates order in the universe. There is tremendous order in nature and in the cosmos, and this is attributed to mahattattva. Creation is not random. Mahat gives the template for the creation of the universe.

tatah—from that mahattattva

ahamkara—the one that is created, the ego, the identification principle. While mahat gives the universal blueprint, as it were, ahamkara is the principle of action. This is a universal action. Mahat provides order, and ahamkara creates activity and makes the universe dynamic.

tasmat shodashakara—out of that ahamkara, sixteen products or evolutes came; out of these sixteen products

panchabhyah—from the five out of the sixteen (the tanmatras)

pancabhutani—the five gross elements evolve out of the five tanmatras

// Out of mulaprakriti, the universal cosmic intelligence (*mahat*) and the ego principle (*ahamkara*), emerge, followed by sixteen evolutes from ahamkara. Out of the sixteen evolutes, five of these create five more evolutes. //

This karika describes the process of evolution. Mahat, the cosmic intelligence principle, arises out of mulaprakriti. Out of mahat comes the universal ahamkara, the prime mover of activity in the universe. Out of ahamkara come the sixteen evolutes. These are the eleven indriyas in the sattvic stream and five in the tamasic or objective stream. Out of these sixteen evolutes emerge the five tanmatras, the subtle elements that create the five gross elements. As Ishvarakrishna explains earlier, the mulaprariti creates one evolute, which is mahat, the intelligence principle. Mahat in turn produces one evolute, ahamkara, the cosmic driving force, or the self-identification or individual ego principle. But unlike the single evolutes that are mahat and ahamkara, the latter creates sixteen offsprings, which are the eleven indriyas on the one hand, and the five tanmatras on the other. The eleven indriyas do not produce any evolutes, but the five tanmatras produce the five gross elements.

Kārikā 23

The nature of the buddhi, or intellect, the first evolute of prakriti, at the individual level

अध्यवसायोबुद्धिर्धर्मोज्ञानंविरागाइश्वर्यम्
सात्त्विकमेतद्रूपंतामसमस्माद्विपर्यस्तम् ॥२३॥

Adhyavasāyobuddhirdharmojñānaṃvirāgāiśvaryam |
sāttvikametadrūpaṃtāmasamasmādviparyastam ||23||

adhyavasaya—deep analysis, to ascertain; like the way land is made cultivable by plowing, the buddhi or intellect analyzes an issue thoroughly and makes it easy for you to find a solution

buddhih—is the function of the buddhi, or intellect

dharma—that which supports something; anything that supports a system is called *dharma*

jnana—understanding the nature of everything, including the nature of yourself; knowledge

viraga—dispassion

aisvarya—siddhis, supernatural powers (also called *vibhuti*)

satvika etat rupam—when the buddhi is sattvic, these are the four directions/forms it can take

tamams asmat—if the buddhi is tamasic (it is lazy and goes in the path of inertia)

viparya—that which is the opposite path of dharma and the other three paths

// Cosmic intelligence, or mahattattva, exists at the universal level; at the individual level it is known as the *buddhi*, the intellect. It is the mind that analyzes (*adhyavasaya*) and thereby determines everything. When the buddhi is sattvic, these are the qualities it reflects: truth and order (*dharma*), knowledge (*jnana*), renunciation (*vairagya*), and sovereignty or supernatural powers or siddhis (*aishvarya*). The opposites of these qualities occur when the buddhi is dominated by tamas. //

Even though the buddhi, or mahat, evolved out of dominant sattva in the mulaprakriti, at the individual level the buddhi can be dominated by sattva or tamas. For instance, if the buddhi is sattvic it will lead to dharma. It will find the ways of having dharmic thoughts and doing dharmic activities. On the other hand, if the buddhi of a person is predominately tamasic, that person will follow an adharmic path, that is, the opposite of dharma. A tamasic buddhi will be unwholesome and will find the means of adharmic activities for the purpose of self-aggrandizement.

When the buddhi is sattvic, it can lead us along the path of dharma; it can analyze and lead us toward knowledge (*jnana*) of the nature of purusha and prakriti; it can lead us to develop dispassion and detachment (*viraga*) from the world; and it can bring siddhis, or special supernatural powers.

If the buddhi is tamasic, the opposite of sattva will result: a negation of the dharma (*adharma*), ignorance (*ajnana*), intense and irrational attachment (*aviraga*), and (*anaishvarya*) servitude.

Here we find the meaning of the word *dharma*, which is called *ishta* ("sought," "wished for," "desired," "cherished") and *purta* ("fulfilling," "rewarding") in ancient texts. *Purta* describes activities done for the upliftment of other beings, things like building and running choultries, which are inns or resting places for pilgrims given for free; digging wells in drought-prone areas;

giving charity to the deserving and needy; and similar virtuous activities that help the practitioner earn merit and allow him or her to go to higher levels and worlds after life. *Ishta* refers to religious or Vedic activities to propitiate the gods per prescribed rituals, which are also considered dharmic activities. Accumulation of virtue (*punya*) by these means are said to help the practitioner reach higher worlds after this lifetime.

Knowledge, *jnana*, is another path a sattvic mind can take, and this is what allows the practitioner to achieve the ultimate goal of liberation, thereby fulfilling the quest of forever transcending the three types of pain. Jnana refers to knowledge of the distinction between purusha and buddhi. Knowing the difference between consciousness and intelligence is jnana.

Viraga is dispassion. The prefix *vi* means here, "without," and *raga* describes an intense infatuation with sense objects. A mind that is detached and dispassionate toward the material world is viraga (and such a state of mind is called *vairagya*). A sattvic buddhi is able to analyze and realize that involvement with sense objects may give some transient pleasure, but overall produces nothing but pain and sorrow. So, a discerning sattvic buddhi will work toward developing viraga through analysis and practice. This reduces attachment and increases dispassion. According to Vyasa writing a commentary on Patanjali's yoga sutra, developing detachment, viraga, involves four progressive stages:

- *yatamana*—the stage of making initial efforts
- *vyatireka*—complete control over one or some of the senses
- *ekendriya*—all senses under control but faint recollection of sense pleasure lingers in the mind
- *vasikara*—senses under complete control and no desire lingers in the mind

The first stage is *yatamana*, making effort. This refers to a conscious effort not to employ the sensory faculties of the eyes, ears, and the organs of speech or sex. When one is successful to an extent at the yatamana stage, attachment to objects of some of the senses are completely eliminated, while others are greatly weakened. After practicing this awhile, there will be a better disposition toward renunciation itself. Maintaining this mental state over time is known as *vyatiraka samjna vairagyam*, basically, knowledge of complete detachment. During this time the senses come completely under the control of the mind, leaving only faint impressions of sense pleasure in the mind. Thereafter, as a result of regular meditation practice, the yogi will be able to eradicate all thoughts of sense pleasure from the mind, and that is the state that Ishvarakrishna is referring to here, the state that Patanjali calls *vasikara*, "complete control."

But this state of detachment from the sensory world still does not lead to liberation, say Ishvarakrishna and Patanjali, as there is no direct perception of the true Self as distinct from the buddhi. Yogis call this *apara vairagya*, meaning a lower level of vairagya. But vairagya, or dispassion, toward all cittavrittis can take place only after the realization of the Self takes place within a sattvic buddhi. And only jnana, knowledge, will lead to this realization.

Morever, a sattvic person will take the path of lordship (*aisvarya*), says Ishvarakrishna. This, along with the development of siddhis, implies enormous supernatural abilities. The eightfold siddhis mentioned in ancient scriptures or the variety of siddhis mentioned by Patanjali in his Yoga Sutras are the result of a sattvic buddhi in a state of samadhi. In fact, samadhi can be achieved only in a sattvic buddhi.

Kārikā 24

The characteristics of self-identification and the subsequent evolution of the universe

अभिमानोऽहङ्कारस्तस्माद्विविधःप्रवर्ततेसर्गः ।
एकादशकश्च गणस्तन्मात्रः पञ्चकश्चैव ॥२४॥

Abhimāno'haṅ kārastasmāddvividhaḥpravartatesargaḥ |
ekādaśakaścagaṇastanmātraḥpañcakaścaiva ||24||

abhimana—repeatedly thinking this body that acts is the true Self and getting passionately attached to it, as opposed to understanding that purusha, the Self, does not act
abhimana—manifest as attachment to the body
Abhimano ahankarah—self-assertion, principle of self-identification
dvididhah—twofold
pravartate—evolves
sargah—stream of evolution
ekadashasya ganah—group of eleven items
tanmatran ca—the subtle forms of the elements (*tanmatras*)
pancakah ca eva—are of five kinds

// Self-identification or ego (*ahamkara*) emerges following the manifestation of the buddhi from mahat tattva, or cosmic intelligence. The cosmic energy of ahamkara, the force that creates enormous activity in the universe, is the motivating force of creation. This macrocosmic ahamkara becomes the

source for the production of eleven indriyas at the microcosmic level and the five tanmatras that are the source of the gross elements that constitute the objective universe. //

Ahamkara at the individual level is self-identification. It involves repeatedly thinking that with this body, the individual "I" can do many things: *I* write books, *I* have a fit body, *I* am rich, *I* am in control . . . However, all these are manifestations of ahamkara, the individual ego. After a while we begin to identify with the material world and own everything at an individual level. We are so deluded by ego that we cannot move beyond it to recognize the true Self. *Aham* means "I," and *kara* is "doer." This contrasts with the Samkhya and Yoga view that purusha, the true Self, is merely a witness and never acts. Ahamkara, self-identification, occurs at the individual level when it is experienced as an emotional attachment to the body and its capabilities (*abhimana*). That is why samkhyas seek to subdue the ego so that sattva and the clarity it brings can rise to the forefront.

Ahamkara is recognized at the universal or cosmic level as well. We have already noted the Samkhya view that the creation is orderly, created after deep contemplation of the mahat, or universal intelligence. But then in the universe there is also activity, enormous, incessant activity. This is attributed to universal ahamkara.

From the universal ahamkara proceed two streams: a sattvic (or subjective) stream, and a tamasic (or objective) stream. The sattvic stream consists of eleven sense faculties: five organs of action (*karmendriyas*), five organs of perception (*jnanendriyas*), and mind (*manas*). The tamasic stream produces the five subtle, rudimentary forms of the elements (*tanmatras*), which further create the five gross elements that become the building blocks of the world. In this way, according to Samkhya, the universal ahamkara makes all the components of the universe act in a particular way by giving the necessary impetus.

So buddhi and ahamkara exist at both the cosmic and the microcosmic levels. The world is divided into beings who are subjects and those that are objects. The subjects are beings with a buddhi, or intellect, and an ego, and eleven sense faculties, which allow one to interact with the objects in the outside world.

Kārikā 25

Rajas guna as a facilitator in the process of evolution

सात्त्विकैकादशकःप्रवर्ततेवैकृतादहङ्कारात् ।
भूतादेस्तन्मात्रः स तामसस्तैजसादुभयम् ॥ २५॥

Sāttvikaikādaśakaḥpravartatevaikṛtādahaṅkārāt |
bhūtādestanmātraḥsatāmasastaijasādubhayam ||25||

satvika ekadashakah—from the ahamkara, eleven sense faculties arise from the sattvic stream of evolution
vaikruta—evolved
ahankarat—from ahamkara
tamasa—tamasic
bhutadeh—elements from the tamasic aspect
tanmatra pravartate—all tanmatras evolve with the presence of tamas
tejasad ubhayam—both streams are evolved and energized by rajas

// From the ahamkara in a sattvic mode, the five indriyas or senses and instruments of action plus the coordinating manas evolve. Then in a tamasic mode the universal ahamkara

produces the five subtle elements, or tanmatras,
thus producing sixteen evolutes. //

In the previous sloka we learned which evolutes of prakriti are either sattvic and which ones are tamasic. The sattvic aspect produces eleven sense faculties; the tamasic aspect produces five rudimentary forms of the elements (the tanmatras), which further produce the five gross elements. This karika says that the production of both of these aspects requires the thrust of rajasic energy.

Both sattva and tamas inherently lack the ability to precipitate change in the universe. Rajas provides the action of transformation to the two aspects of ahamkara, sattvic and tamasic, to manifest as entities embodying their respective qualities: from the sattvic aspect emerges the eleven sense faculties, and from the tamasic aspect come the five tanmatras.

Kārikā 26

The ten sense faculties, or indriyas

बुद्धीन्द्रियाणिचक्षुःश्रोत्रघ्राणरसनत्वगाख्यानि ।
वाक्पाणिपादपायूपस्थान्कर्मेन्द्रियान्याहुः ॥२६॥

Buddhīndriyāṇicakṣuḥśrotraghrāṇarasanatvagākhyāni |
vākpāṇipādapāyūpasthānkarmendriyānyāhuḥ ||26||

buddhindriyani—senses of perception (*jnanendriyas*)
caksu—eyes
shrotra—ears
ghrana—nose

rasana—tongue
sparshana—skin, tactile sensation
vak—speech
pani—arms
pada—legs
payu—excretory organ
upastha—generative organ

// The sense organs that deal with perception, the *jnanendriyas*, are the eyes, ears, nose, tongue, and skin. We take in information from the outside world through these sense organs. The action instruments that deal with bodily functions and actions are the *karmendriyas*. They are the tongue,* the arms, the legs, the excretory organ, and the generative organ. They act on the outside world. //

The five subtle elements, or *tanmatras*, create the five elements, or *bhutas*. And the five bhutas act as the mediums for each of the subtle elements. The tanmatras emanating from objects or entities traverse through their respective medium and reach their respective sense organ, to then be grasped and transmitted to the brain (*citta*). *Rupa tanmatra*, or light particles, traverse the fire (*agni*) element and are grasped by the eyes (*cakshurindriya*), while the mind (*manas*) deciphers the object. Likewise, *sabda tanmatra*, or sound waves, traverse the medium of space (*akasa*), are grasped by the ears (*shrotra*) and sent to the mind (*manas*) in order to recognize the sound. In a similar fashion, the other subtle sense faculties, or tanmatras, traverse through their respective mediums to reach their respective sense organ, to be grasped and decoded by the mind (manas).

---

*Ishvarakrishna later points out that the tongue has duel functions: to taste food and to speak, hence it is both a jnanendriya and a karmendriya.

Kārikā 27

The nature of the mind, or manas,
the eleventh sense organ

उभयात्मकमत्रमनःसङ्कल्पकमिन्द्रियं च साधर्म्यात् ।
गुणपरिणामविशेषान्नानात्वंबाह्यभेदाच्च ॥२७॥

Ubhayātmakamatramanaḥsaḥkalpakamindriyaṃ ca sādharmyāt |
guṇapariṇāmaviśeṣānnānātvaṃbāhyabhedācca ||27||

ubhayatmakam—for both the organs of action (*karmendriyas*) and the organs of perception (*jnanendriyas*)
atra—in that group of the eleven sense organs (*indriyas*)
manah—mind, the eleventh sense organ, which coordinates karmendriyas and jnanendriyas
guna parinama visesaat—objects that are seen differently due to the activities of the three gunas
sadharmyam ca indriyan ca—on account of mind having commonality with the other sense organs
samkalpakam indriyam—the determining sense organ, or indriya

// Here the eleventh of the sense organs, the mind, or manas, is taken up for discussion. The mind is an organ like the other sense organs, but it belongs to both the organs of action, the karmendriyas, and those of perception, the jnanendriyas. Both the jnanendriyas and the karmendriyas act because of the coordination afforded by the mind, or manas. //

The information we get from the outside world through the senses is coordinated by the mind, considered the eleventh sense organ according to Samkhya. Many things that happen in the body are done directly by the mind without it going through the intellect (the buddhi) and the ego (the ahamkara). It analyzes, ponders. Therefore, on account of its similarity with the other ten indriyas it is also called a sense organ, an indriya. Different objects are seen differently due to the balance of the gunas, and these in turn are grasped by the senses.

Kārikā 28

The functions of the five organs of perception and the five organs of action

शब्दादिषुपञ्चानामालोचनमात्रमिष्यतेवृत्तिः ।
वचनादानविहरणोत्सर्गानन्दाश्चपञ्चानाम् ॥२८॥

Sabdādiṣupañcānāmālocanamātramiṣyatevṛttiḥ |
vacanādānaviharaṇotsargānandāścapañcānām ||28||

panchanam—the five senses
sabdadishu—in sound and others
alochana vrittihi matram—capable of the activity of observing only
vacana—to speak
adana—to grasp
viharana—to walk
utsarga—to excrete
ananda—to produce pleasure
pancanam—the five functions of the organs of action

// The five instruments of perception, the jnanendriyas, are the ears for hearing (*sabda*), the skin for touching (*sparsa*), the eyes for seeing (*rupa*), the tongue for tasting (*rasa*), and the nose for smelling (*gandha*). These sense organs are capable of observing or grasping only. They are there only to transmit information, and they rely on the mind, the manas, to interpret. The mind cannot observe without the senses, but the senses themselves do not see, they only transmit from the outside. The five instruments of action, the karmendriyas, are speech (*vacana*), grasping (*adana*), walking (*viharana*), excreting (*utsarjana*), and the organ of pleasure (*ananda*). //

The instruments of perception, the jnanendriyas, receive information from the outside world. The five instruments of action, the karmendriyas, in turn act in the outside world.

Kārikā 29

Prana and the three evolutes of the mind

स्वालक्षण्यंवृत्तिस्त्रयस्यसैषाभवत्यसामान्या ।
सामान्यकरणवृत्तिःप्राणाद्यावायवःपञ्च ॥२९॥

Svālakṣaṇyaṃvṛttistrayasyasaiṣābhavatyasāmānyā |
sāmānyakaraṇavṛttiḥprāṇādyāvāyavaḥpañca ||29||

svaalakshanyam—individual inherent characteristic
vritti—activity, functions, modifications
trayasya—of the three (referring to the buddhi, the ahamkara, and the manas)
sa esha—with this

asamanya—unique, uncommon
samanyakarana vritti—the common functions of the group of three (buddhi, ahamkara, and manas), collectively called *antahkarana* or *citta*
panchavayavah—the five winds (*vayus*, or prana)
pranadyah—prana and the others

// The mind (*manas*), intellect (*buddhi*), and ego (*ahamkara*) together are generally called *citta*, meaning that which appears to have consciousness (*cit iva bhavayati iti cittam*). These internal instruments are called *antahkarana* and have their own characteristic functions. But then there is a function common to all three (*samanya karana vritti*), which are the five winds or vayus, commonly known as the five aspects of *prana*. //

There are five forces responsible for maintaining life:

- *prana*—inhalation
- *apana*—exhalation
- *vyana*—air and nutrients diffused throughout the body
- *udana*—supporting the organs above the heart
- *samana*—digestion

According to this sloka, the life force, prana, is a function of the intellect (buddhi), the ego (ahamkara), and the mind (manas), which are the inner faculties, or *antahkarana*. This Patanjali calls the *citta*. This implies that life function through the pranas is due to the general activity of the brain, or citta. Here, Ishvarakrishna finds the differences between these three components of the mind as well as the function they have in common. Patanjali's cittavrittis, or thoughts, are not the common activity. Thoughts change from moment to moment and are entirely different from person to person. Here cittavrittis include mental dispositions (*manovritti*), egoic attitudes (*ahamkara-vritti*), and intellectual dispositions (*buddhivritti*), all of which

Patanjali classifies as *cittavritties*. When Patanjali speaks of *citta vritti nirodha*, he is referring to stopping specific cittavrittis. But the universal or general vritti (*samanya*) of citta that samkhyas refer to in this sloka is that which maintains life through the circulation of prana. So when the cessation of thoughts, *citta vritti nirodha*, takes place, only the thought vrittis are stopped and not prana, the life force. The yogi continues to live a sedate life until prana ceases and leaves the body at the time of death.

Kārikā 30

Coordination between the senses, the mind, the ego, and the intellect

युगपच्चतुष्टयस्यतुवृत्तिःक्रमशश्चतस्यनिर्दिष्टा ।
दृष्टेतथाप्यदृष्टेत्रयस्यतत्पूर्विकावृत्तिः ॥३०॥

Yugapaccatuṣṭayasyatuvṛttiḥkramaśaścatasyanirdiṣṭā |
dṛṣṭetathāpyadṛṣṭetrayasyatatpūrvikāvṛttiḥ ||30||

yugapat—simultaneously
catushtasya tasya—foursome
tu—surely
vritti—activity
kramasasca—in sequence
nirdishta—is said conclusively
drshte—the seen, engaging the senses with an object of the senses
tathapi—further
adrshte—cannot be seen, subtle
trayasya—of the three, three internal organs

// When we engage the senses with an object, four aspects are involved: one or more of the sense organs, the mind, the ego, and the intellect. These four are activated either simultaneously or in succession. But even when the senses are not engaged, the totality of the mind (*antahkarana*) can still be active. //

When we see an object, the eyes are engaged, information is grasped and sent inward, the mind coordinates it, gives it to the ego, which determines whether "I like it" or "I don't like it, while the intellect analyzes the whole thing. This composite picture is then presented to the purusha to simply witness.

But when one is not engaged in an outside activity or is sitting with eyes closed in a secluded place, meditating, the totality of the mind (*antahkarana*), including all three (buddhi, ahamkara, and manas) of these aspects, can still be active. In the case of a yogi sitting in meditation, outside objects as perceived by their respective senses are not engaged, although the totality of the mind is still involved. Even so, the mind gets less and less involved in engaging with the external world. The ego, the ahamkara, weakens as the intellect, the buddhi, is engrossed in uplifting thoughts, until the buddhi is able to focus on only one object, to the point of forgetting one's own body. That state of focused vritti is samadhi.

Kārikā 31

The function of the sense faculties as thoughts that present to the purusha

स्वांस्वांप्रतिपद्यन्तेपरस्पराकूतहेतुकांवृत्तिम् ।
पुरुषार्थैवहेतुर्नकेनचित्कार्यतेकरणम् ॥३१॥

Svāṃsvāṃpratipadyanteparasparākūtahetukāṃvṛttim |
puruṣārthaivaheturnakenacitkāryatekaraṇam ||31||

karanani, karanam—the organs of cause (the organs of perception and organs of action)
paraspara—mutually
aakuta—impel, excite, help
hetukaam—the organs help one another, absolute coordination
vritti—activity
purushartha hetukam—whole purpose is to satisfy the purusha
kenachit—by whatever, for no other purpose than to do for one's own satisfaction

// The organs help one another and mutually stimulate one another. They perform their respective functions in response to their corresponding sense organs, and do this only for the purpose of satisfying oneself. They are but servants to oneself. //

We do everything for the need and purpose of the ego, thinking of it as the purusha, but unfortunately without knowing what constitutes the Self or knowing that the purusha does not need anything.

Kārikā 32

The thirteen sense faculties that act to deliver experiences to the purusha

करणंत्रयोदशविधं तदाहरण१धारणप्रकाशकरम् ।
कार्यं च तस्यदशधाहार्यंधार्यंप्रकाश्यं च ॥३२॥

Karaṇaṃtrayodaśavidhaṃtadāharaṇadhāraṇaprakāśakaram |
kāryaṃ ca tasyadaśadhāhāryaṃdhāryaṃprakāśyaṃ ca ||32||

karanam—things that act, organs of causation
triyodasavidham—within us are thirteen organs of causation—five karmendriyas, five jnanendriyas, and the three aspects that comprise the totality of the mind (the *antahkarana*): manas, buddhi, and ahankara
tat—that, the antahkarana (the collective of buddhi, ahamkara, and manas)
aharana—to grasp
dharana—to hold
prakashakam—to clarify or illuminate
karyam—to act
dashadhaharyam—karmendriyas and jnanendriyas together are of ten types

// The sense faculties number thirteen: five karmendriyas (organs of action), five jnanendriyas (organs of perception), and three aspects of the mind/brain (the *antahkarana*—manas, buddhi, and ahankara). They grasp, hold, and clarify or illuminate objects. //

The way in which we perceive an object is explained in this sloka. There are thirteen organs of causation (*karanas*). The manas, the mind, grasps the object, with all its attributes transmitted by the senses. Then it is given to the ahamkara, the individual ego, which holds it and colors it. It then goes to buddhi, the intellect, which clarifies it completely. This process goes on continuously. Then the final cittavritties are presented to the purusha, which merely experiences.

One might wonder how the buddhi, the intellect, which is

part of prakriti and has no consciousness on its own, can reveal consciousness. What is consciousness? Who or what can reveal it? That is the job of the intellect, which can only show the difference (*viveka*) between consciousness, or *cit*, and the mind/brain, or *citta*. Buddhi is that which illuminates and clarifies, but it does so without consciousness or awareness. In fact, it can clarify so many things, just the way a computer can clarify. This electronic device immediately points out my spelling and grammar mistakes. I believe that it has no awareness of what it does; it simply illuminates while in the process of analyzing (*adhyavasaya*). So, you can use your buddhi in service to dharma, to spiritual power and truth, or to *adharma*, that which is not in accord with dharma. So the buddhi can do any of these things, but to achieve ultimate liberation you can only use your buddhi for jnana, knowledge, which will eventually lead to kaivalya.

Kārikā 33

The internal and external instruments of action

अन्तःकरणंत्रिविधंदशधाबाह्यंत्रयस्यविषयाख्यम् ।
साम्प्रतकालंबाह्यं त्रिकालमाभ्य१न्तरं करणम् ॥३३॥

Antaḥkaraṇaṃtrividhaṃdaśadhābāhyaṃtrayasyaviṣayākhyam |
sāmpratakālaṃbāhyaṃ trikālamābhya1ntaraṃ karaṃam ||33||

antahkaranam—the internal organ
trividam—of three types or of three aspects: manas, ahamkara, and buddhi
dashadha—of ten types

bahyam—external faculties are the karmendriyas and the jnanendriyas
vishayakyam—those that are known as objects
samprata kalam—they act at a particular moment, the present
bahyam—external organs
trikala—function all the three times, future, present, and past
abhyantaram karanam—the three internal organs

// The external organs number ten (the five karmendriyas and the five jnanendriyas); they act only in the present moment to ultimately reveal to the purusha after processing by the antahkarana, the combined internal organs consisting of the buddhi, the ahamkara, and the manas. They receive from the external organs and can function with reference to all three times, past, present, and future. //

The external organs can operate only in the present moment, whereas the internal organs can operate in all three times: they can think of the past, think of the future, and operate in the present moment. The internal organs process what is received from the external organs and present to the purusha.

Kārikā 34

The relationship between the three aspects of the mind and the five organs of perception

बुद्धीन्द्रियाणितेषांपञ्चविशेषाविशेषविषयाणि ।
वाग्भवतिशब्दविषयाशेषाणितु पञ्चविषयाणि१ ॥३४॥

Buddhīndriyāṇiteṣāṃpañcaviśeṣāviśeṣaviṣayāṇi |
vāgbhavatiśabdaviṣayāśeṣāṇitupañcaviṣayāṇi ||34||

buddhi indriyani—the sense organs
tesham—of the three
visesha avihesha vishayani—the objects are specific or nonspecific, gross or subtle
vag bhavathi—the *vak*, or tongue, is both a karmendriya and a jnanendriya
shabdavishaya—for the purpose of speech
shehsani—the others are the specific objects

// The three aspects of the mind (manas, buddhi, and akamkara), and the five organs of perception are specific or nonspecific, gross or subtle. The tongue pertains to both the jnanendriyas and the karmendriyas. //

The five organs of perception, the jnanendriyas, attend to sounds, forms, smells, tactile sensations, and taste. The tongue, which is the organ of taste, doubles as a karmendriya, the organ of speech. The objects of the perceptual senses according to this sloka are of two types, called *visesha* and *avisesha*. *Visesha* refers to gross objects that are ordinarily accessed by the senses. For example, as an ordinary person, my eyesight is limited to a particular range and particular dimensions. If the object is too small or too far away, I cannot see it. Likewise for the other senses. I can hear only if the sound is above a particular decibel level, and so forth for the other jnanendriyas. However, here Ishvarakrishna talks about the objects of the senses being *avisesha*, or as subtle as the tanmatras, the rudimentary elements from which the gross elements are formed. While ordinary people like us have a very narrow range of sensory perception, yogis are able to sense objects that are very subtle and even divine, which is represented by the term *avisesha*. In his Yoga Sutras (3.42), Patanjali refers to hearing divine sounds:

Srotrakasayoh sambandha samyamath divyam srotram

By samyama, or concentrating, on the relationship between space and the power of hearing, the higher, divine power of hearing comes.

The siddha yogi who by intense samadhi is able to discern the connection between the hearing instrument, or the ear, and akasa, or space (the medium through which sound, both audible and subtle, is said to travel according to Samkhya and Yoga) is able to hear divine sayings and sounds. It is generally said that the Vedic mantras were revealed to the rishis due to their intense yogic powers. These subtle sensory perceptions can be used for control of the citta (*vishayavati va pravritti utpanna manasah sthiti nibhandini*). According to Patanjali, by samyama, or yogic contemplation on subtle sensations, one can achieve enormous control over the mind.

My guru would say that of all the senses, the tongue is most difficult to control. It creates *capalya*, craving in a person. This craving of the tongue is called *juhva capalya*, "weakness of the tongue." The tongue has a weakness for tasty food, which in all probability will not be wholesome. The other weakness for the tongue involves speech. This becomes a weakness if the antahkarana, the three aspects of the mind, especially the buddhi, is not fully engaged, in which case the tongue, if uncontrolled by a sattvic buddhi, can lead one to avoidable trouble with the outside world.

Kārikā 35

The buddhi processes information presented by the senses, and like a gatekeeper presents it to the purusha. The other sense organs are only gates.

सान्तःकरणाबुद्धिःसर्वंविषयमवगाहतेयस्मात् ।
तस्मात्त्रिविधंकरणंद्वारिद्वाराणिशेषाणि ॥३५॥

Sāntaḥkaraṇābuddhiḥsarvaṃviṣayamavagāhateyasmāt |
tasmāttrividhaṃkaraṇaṃdvāridvārāṇiśeṣāṇi ||35||

yasmat—because
santahkarana—with the other internal organs
buddhi—the intellect
sarvam visayam—all the things
avagahate—is able to comprehend
tasmat—therefore
trividha karanam—three types of aspects (or the three aspects of the mind/brain)
dvari—gatekeepers
sesani dvarani—rest of the sense faculties are only gates

// The buddhi is able to comprehend all things with the assistance of the manas, the mind, and the ahamkara, the ego. Therefore, these three aspects—buddhi, manas, and ahamkara (the three collectively known as the *antahkarana*)—are considered gatekeepers, allowing processed information to be presented as a cittavritti for the purusha to witness. Before everything is presented to the purusha (or when one becomes aware of an experience in the mind), these three aspects coordinate and process the information received. The rest of the karmendriyas and jnanendriyas are only gates. //

The buddhi is the most important faculty in a person, whether for understanding worldly and otherworldly matters or when pertaining to one's true Self, the purusha. The sense faculties are special gates that permit what each one is designed to permit. The antahkarana processes the information, colors it appropriately, and the final cittavritti is witnessed by the seer, the purusha. Buddhi is intelligence, purusha is consciousness. They are different—the former provides the object, and the latter is the subject.

Kārikā 36

Disparate elements but one common goal

एतेप्रदीपकल्पाःपरस्परविलक्षणागुणविशेषाः ।
कृत्स्नंपुरुषस्यार्थंप्रकाश्यबुद्धौप्रयच्छन्ति ॥३६॥

Etepradīpakalpāḥparasparavilakṣaṇāguṇaviśeṣāḥ |
kṛtsnaṃpuruṣasyārthaṃprakāśyabuddhauprayacchanti ||36||

pradīpakalpāḥ—like a lamp
paraspara vilakshanah—differing from one another
ete—these
gunavisesa—objects of differing gunas
purusasyartam—for the sake of purusha
kritsnam—fully and entirely, the gunas work only for the sake of purusha
prakasya—clarifying everything
buddhau prayachanti—presents to buddhi ultimately for the sake of purusha

// Like the constituents of an oil lamp that differ from one another (oil, wick, and flame), the gunas, even though they differ from one another, work, as if, on behalf of the purusha fully and entirely. Everything gathered by the senses is presented to the buddhi to be witnessed by the purusha. //

Information comes from the outside world through the senses; the manas grasps it, the ahamkara colors it, and the buddhi analyzes it, and in this way the three gunas come into play. If the buddhi is sattvic, it makes an agreeable presentation, while the manas collates and coordinates, the ahamkara further colors it. Ultimately, all three of them make a presentation to the purusha. The same information will be colored differently by the antahkarana, depending on the dominance of one of the three gunas. This explains the process of knowing.

Kārikā 37

The buddhi is the most important faculty for achieving kaivalya.

सर्वंप्रत्युपभोगंयस्मात्पुरुषस्यसाधयतिबुद्धिः ।
सैव च विशिनष्टि पुनः१ प्रधानपुरुषान्तरंसूक्ष्मम् ॥३७॥

Sarvaṃpratyupabhogaṃyasmātpuruṣasyasādhayatibuddhiḥ |
saiva ca viśinaṣṭipunaḥpradhānapuruṣāntaraṃsūkṣmam ||37||

yasmat—because of
buddhih—the intellect
sarvamprati—about all matters
upabhogam—experience
purusasya—for the purusha
sadhayati—accomplishes
sa eva—the same buddhi
sukshmam—the subtle
pradhana purushantaram—the distinction between prakriti and purusha
visinashti—clearly reveals (in a yogi)

// Because the buddhi controls the ahamkara and all the other senses, it can clarify everything. The buddhi is that which enables all the experiences that are taking place to be experienced by purusha. The same buddhi that presents everything to purusha is the same faculty that is the one capable of revealing the distinction between purusha and prakriti. //

The buddhi commonly gives the erroneous belief that the brain, or citta, has consciousness; but when in a sattvic yogic mode it shows the difference between consciousness and the brain to the purusha. When this realization takes place, the buddhi will withdraw, fully satisfied that it has nothing more to do. Why so? The buddhi is able to directly realize that the unchanging purusha can be made neither happy nor unhappy. All the feverish activities of the senses as well as the antahkarana are absolutely futile and unnecessary. I, the unenlightened I, do everything to make "me" happy and remove unhappiness. But when my buddhi realizes that the purusha, the Self, does not require anything to make it happy or unhappy, my buddhi is fully satisfied and will reach a state of absolute peace.

The Yoga Sutras (2.18) say,

Prakasa kriya sthiti silam bhutendriyatmakam
bhogapavargartham drshyam

The seen individual person possesses clarity, activity, and inertia (manifestation of the three gunas). That entity consists of the five gross and five subtle elements and organs or indriyas. Its purpose is to get worldly experience and the ultimate release (of the Self).

The manifest individual human being is made of the three gunas, whose effects are clarity, activity, and restraint. This human being has also the five subtle and gross elements, or bhutas, and eleven indriyas along with ego and intelligence. What can one do with these during one's lifetime? They can be used for different kinds of experiences (*bhoga*), which the prakriti or the outside world offer. It is *apavarga*. *Varga* means "progression" or "expansion." The prefix *apa* gives the opposite meaning, which is to regress. It means the yogi contemplates all twenty-four prakritic tattvas in his or her own prakritic body-mind to arrive at the determination that it is not the Self. In this process of reverse meditation, the yogi arrives at the truth of the Self. So, two paths are open for all human beings—more and more worldly or otherworldly experiences, or an apavarga approach such as this, to reach the real nature of the Self and attain permanent relief from the three sources of pain and sorrow. The same yogi is called *drishya*, or the physical person seen as the individual/self, in the Yoga Sutras. *Bhoga* implies various experiences—good, bad, indifferent, mixed, and apavarga. Apavarga is to overcome any misunderstandings of the twenty-four prakritic tattvas through the yogic process of concentration or samyama, and then *citta vritti nirodha* takes place. Both of them, the various experiences, or bhoga, and the final release (apavarga) are possible. Each one of us has to do this individually, nobody else will do this for us. We each have the necessary capacity, the inherent tools, the yogic tools. The capacity is found in the form of the buddhi, the intellect or brain; how we use the buddhi is what determines the outcome. If you can train it, it will show you the difference between prakriti and purusha. But first the buddhi must be in a sattvic mode and directed in the jnana course of seeking knowledge.

Kārikā 38

The macrocosmic evolution from the subtle elements to the physical elements

तन्मात्राण्यविशेषास्तेभ्योभूतानिपञ्चपञ्चभ्यः ।
एतेस्मृताविशेषाःशान्ताघोराश्चमूढाश्च ॥ ३८॥

Tanmātrāṇyaviśeṣāstebhyobhūtānipañcapañcabhyaḥ |
etesmṛtāviśeṣāḥśāntāghorāścamūḍhāśca ||38||

tanmatrani—the tanmatras as pure sense stimulators
avisesah—subtle, indistinguishable
tebhyah pancabhyah—from the five tanmatras, or subtle elements
bhutani—the five gross elements, or bhutas, evolve
ete—these
bhutah—bhutas, gross elements
santah—calm, sattva
ghorah—violent, rajas
mudhah—heavy, tamas
visesah—the distinguishable

// From the subtle elements, or tanmatras—hearing (*sabda*), touching (*sparsa*), seeing (*rupa*), tasting (*rasa*), and smelling (*gandha*)—the five gross aspects of evolution (earth, air, fire, water, and space) are produced. *Avisesa*, "subtle," here refers to the tanmatras; *visesa*, "distinguishable" or "gross," refers to the bhutas. //

In the last stage of the evolution of objects at the macrocosmic level we have the five tanmatras that produce five different bhutas and their combinations; and in the different proportions of the gunas we find innumerable objects that express the three different qualities. Some are predominantly sattvic or calm (santa), others are predominantly rajasic or aggressive (ghora), and then some tamasic or dull (mudha). The multitude of objects are constituted by the bhutas and permeated by the gunas. The different proportions of the gunas and in the gross elements make for an infinite number of objects in the universe.

Kārikā 39

The three bodies: subtle, gross, and genetic

सूक्ष्मामातापितृजाःसहप्रभूतैस्त्रिधाविशेषाःस्युः ।
सूक्ष्मास्तेषांनियतामातापितृजानिवर्तन्ते ॥३९॥

Sūkṣmāmātāpitṛjāḥsahaprabhūtaistridhāviśeṣāḥsyuḥ |
sūkṣmāsteṣāṃniyatāmātāpitṛjānivartante ||39||

suksmah, suksmasarira—the subtle body
matapitruhah—the (body) given by the parents
saha—together with
prabhuta bhutasarira—the physical body
tridhasyuh—three body types are there
suksmah tesam niyata, suksma sarira—will not die, it migrates and stays until the final dissolution or state of kaivalya
matapitrja nivartante—the genetic body provided by the mother and father and the gross body that arises out of the parental body, perish

// We have three bodies. Two of them, the physical body and the genetic body produced by the parents, go away at the end of life. At the time of death, the subtle body with its karma bundle also leaves the body. The embryonic or genetic body is provided by the parents, each contributing an egg and a sperm containing the genes. This is called *mata pitruja sarira* or body given by the mother and father. //

The physical body consists of the five elements in different combinations. All these five bhutas will merge back into the original constituents, the five bhutas or gross elements, upon death. Commentators refer to the dead body being eaten by animals or buried or cremated, at which point it is finally reduced to the five bhutas. So, the corpse (*bhuta sarira*) is reduced to the five basic gross elements. The subtle body (*suksmasarira*) will not release if you are a *baddha atma*, one still in bondage due to ignorance of the nature of the Self, as during the final dissolution it will merge into the mulaprakriti. When the next incarnation starts, the same subtle body will continue to operate. If there is kaivalya, however, the subtle body will not transmigrate; it will merge into the mulaprakriti.

The Yoga Sutras (2.13) say,

Sati mule tad vipako jatiayur bhogah

As long as avidya or ignorance of the Self exists, the karma bundle will fructify and produce another birth of a different species, lifespan, and experiences.

This sutra indicates that as long as a person has unripened karma in their karma bundle and has not eradicated ignorance (*avidya*) of the nature of the Self, the individual will transmigrate and take another birth and suffer the three causes of pain for a stipulated life span. It may be of interest to note that samkhyas introduce a body called the genetic body (*matapitruja sarira*). While the subtle body (*sukshma sarira*) carries the old karma bundle, the genetic body gives the individual characteristics within the species. The genetic body is found in the embryo (it carries the genetic characteristics of *mata* and *pita*, or mother and father), which ingests food from the mother and develops a physical body (bhuta sarira) as a fetus.

Kārikā 40

Subtle body characteristics

पूर्वोत्पन्नमसक्तंनियतंमहदादिसूक्ष्मपर्यन्तम् ।
संसरतिनिरुपभोगंभावैरधिवासितंलिङ्गम् ॥४०॥

Pūrvotpannamasaktaṃniyataṃmahadādisūkṣmaparyantam |
saṃsaratinirupabhogaṃbhāvairadhivāsitaṃliṅgam ||40||

lingam, *lingasarira*—the subtle body
purvautpannam—that was created in the beginning itself
asakta—unimpeded
niyatam—permanent, existing until final dissolution
mahadadi—referring to mahat, ahamkara, and manas
sukshma paryantam—including the subtle tanmatras
samsarati—transmigrates
nirupa bhogam—it doesn't experience (the purusha is the experiencer)
bhava—past karmas
adhivasitam—are stored here, the storage

// The subtle body is so called because it cannot be perceived by the senses. It is created at the beginning of the prakritic evolution. It is subtle because it ultimately merges with the mulaprakriti. It transmigrates birth after birth until the final dissolution takes place, or until the person attains kaivalya, or permanent freedom. //

The subtle body, without the capacity to employ sensory faculties, was created at the beginning of evolution when the mulaprakriti began to evolute. It has the capacity to move anywhere unimpeded. It is constant; it cannot be modified. It consists of mahat (cosmic intelligence), ahamkara (self-identification), manas (mind), the ten indriyas, and the five rudimentary subtle elements that are the tanmatras. Even though it's a subtle body, it doesn't experience, it is inert. Experience is given to the purusha. The subtle body is where past karmas are stored and carried to the next rebirth in the process of transmigration.

The Yoga Sutras (2.12) say,

Klesamulah karmasayo drsta adrsta janma vedaniyah

As long as the main klesha, the cause of pain or ignorance of the nature of the Self, is not eradicated, the subtle body, along with the bundle of unripened past karmas, will transmigrate.

A mantra that directly explains the essentials of Samkhya is found in the Mahanarayana Upanishad:

Ajamekamlohitaśuklakriśnam| bahvhimprajāmjanayantisarupām ajohyekojuśamano 'nuśete| jahāhātyenāmbhukta-bhogāmajo 'nyah

Let's break this down further:

Aja means "without birth," and *ja* (or *janma*) means "birth." Mulaprakriti is a prakriti or producer, not a *vikriti* or evolute—it is not created from something else. The Sanskrit *ajam* (unborn) and *ekam* (one) mean "there is one that is unborn." *Loha* means "metal," specifically iron, and iron produces compounds that are red, so *lohita* refers to a red color. *Shukla* is "white," and *krishna* is "black." So, the unborn one is of three hues—red, white, and black. These three colors respectively refer to rajas, sattva, and tamas.

Bahvim prajam janayantim sarupam means "It produces many offspring, and all of them also have the same three colors." Here "colors" refers to the three qualities, sattva, rajas and tamas.

Ajoheko jushamanah anushayate means "So it is now pictured like a tree, and in the tree there are plenty of fruits that possess the same three qualities as the tree. In that tree there are two birds sitting on separate branches. One bird is very enthusiastically eating the fruits, enjoying the fruits of the prakriti, like all of us."

Jahatyenam bhukta-bhogam ajo 'nyah means "Another one, having seen that there is nothing else to enjoy in this tree, sits there without enjoying the fruits of the prakriti tree."

The above mantra is found in the last chapter of the Mahanarayana Upanishad. It beautifully and succinctly brings out the essence and goal of Samkhya philosophy. Because this mantra is found in the Vedas, many scholars call Samkhya a Vedic philosophy. The rishi or sage who discovered this mantra uses a lovely metaphor. It depicts a tree, a very old, massive tree whose beginning cannot be traced. It has several branches. It is said to exhibit three colors, red, white, and black. It bears many fruits of the same colors, say a red skin, white pulp, and dark seeds. On the branches are perched many birds. The mantra takes up the condition of two birds for discussion. One bird is busy eating a fruit. The other bird sitting on another branch does not eat any of the many fruits hanging from the tree and appears to consider the fruits as forbidden.

The tree with three colors and its expansive nature is compared to the prakriti and its three gunas. The red color indicates the rajas guna, the white sattva, and the black tamas. The fruits that the tree bears are also of the same colors, indicating that the evolutes of prakriti possess the three gunas. The one bird that is busy eating fruit is a *baddha atma*, or one still in bondage. The other bird, having seen the nature of the tree and its fruits of different tastes and colors, refrains from having anything to do with the fruits of the tree. That bird is compared to the person who is free, or in the state of kaivalya experienced by a consummate yogi. The two beings, one free and the other (along with a number of others) are still in bondage, tied to the bittersweet fruits of the tree.

Modified forms of this mantra can also be found in some yoga texts and a few other Upanishad texts.

Kārikā 41

The transmigration of the subtle body

चित्रंयथाश्रयमृतेस्थाण्वादिभ्योविनायथाच्छाया ।
तद्वद्विनाविशेषैर्नतिष्ठतिनिराश्रयंलिङ्गम् ॥४१॥

Citraṃyathāśrayamṛtesthāṇvādibhyovināyathāchāyā |
tadvadvināviśeṣairnatiṣṭhatinirāśrayaṃliṅgam ||41||

yatah—just as, in the same way
ashrayarite vina—without support like a wall
citram—a painting (cannot stand)
sthanuadhibhyah vina—without a pillar or another
chaya—a shadow (cannot exist)
Tadvat—likewise
vina aviseshaih—without the tanmatras
lingam—the subtle body
na tishtati—does not stand
nirasraya—as it becomes unsupported

// Just as a painting cannot be displayed without a proper support, or just as a shadow cannot be produced without an object to create it, in the same way, without the tanmatras, the subtle body cannot transmigrate. //

The subtle body (*suksma sarira*) needs a support in order to come into existence. The objective stream consisting of the five elements and the subjective stream of thirteen sense organs are connected by the tanmatras, the rudimentary subtle elements. The tanmatras of objects consisting of the five elements use those elements as the respective mediums to be grasped by their respective senses. According to this sloka, the tanmatras form part of the transmigrating subtle body.

Some philosophers say that there are thirteen constituents of the subtle body: the intellect (buddhi), the ego (ahamkara), the mind (manas), and the five organs of action (karmendriyas) and the five organs of perception (jnanendriyas). Here Ishvarakrishna justifies the inclusion of the five tanmatras in the subtle body as the supporting structure for the inner sense faculties, which together form the subtle body.

Question: Is the subtle body the same as the *jivatma*, the atman of a living being?
Answer: *Jivatma* is a term that is used in some schools of Vedanta and may be comparable to the purusha or the subject. Subtle body refers to a product of prakriti. This is not a term used in Samkhya, which recognizes the unique, individual purushas of each being.

Kārikā 42

The subtle body taking different births or roles, like a stage actor

पुरुषार्थहेतुकमिदंनिमित्तनैमित्तिकप्रसङ्गेन ।
प्रकृतेर्विभुत्वयोगान्नटवद्व्यवतिष्ठतेलिङ्गम् ॥४२॥

Puruṣārthahetukamidaṃnimittanaimittikaprasaṅgena |
prakṛtervibhutvayogānnaṭavadvyavatiṣṭhateliṅgam ||42||

purusartha hetuka—for the sake of attaining the ultimate goal of kaivalya or freedom
idam lingam—this subtle body
nimitta—karmas as a cause of rebirth, instrumental cause
naimittika—the new birth, the effect of a cause
prasangena—association
vibhutvaprakrti—because of the vastness of this universe
natavath—just like a performer, is able to take different roles
lingam—the subtle body is able to find the appropriate role

// Just like the way an actor takes on different roles and plays them, the subtle body takes different gross bodies and acts differently, birth after birth. For the sake of attaining the ultimate goal, and also for giving experiences to the purusha, this subtle body is able to find the appropriate "role," i.e., birth, due to past karmas. //

The purusha is constrained to experience the drama generated by the individual mind or citta. As the Yoga Sutras (2.13) succinctly say,

Sati mule tad vipako jati ayuh bhogah

***If the roots of karma exist,* they ripen and result in the body into which you are born, and the fruits of this karma are experienced throughout the lifetime.**

This sloka has slightly different possible interpretations because of the two terms *purusartha* and *natavat*. The term *purusartha* is a common Sanskrit word used extensively to refer to the four goals of human life that are well-known: *dharma* or righteousness, *artha* or prosperity, *kama* or love and pleasure, and *moksha* or liberation. The word *purusha*, on the other hand, is used primarly in schools such as Yoga, Samkhya, and Vedanta to refer to the unchanging, immortal Self (although in common parlance *purusha* is sometimes used to indicate a human being). *Natavat*, referring to a performer who acts out different roles, implies that the subtle body takes different forms, or roles, in different births and acts accordingly. Here by using the term *purusartha*, only the human birth is indicated, as only in a human life can one attain complete liberation, kaivalya.

As we know, the entire universe is made of the three gunas: sattva, rajas, and tamas. These permeate everything. Due to the preponderance of one of the gunas in each person, different people will follow different goals. Even as everyone's desire is to be happy and eliminate unhappiness, each one, depending on his or her guna temperament, pursues different means and goals for one's satisfaction or happiness. Of the four purusarthas, those whose personality is predominantly sattvic follow dharma as a goal. Dharma is the law of piety, compassion, and orderly life. These people follow the benevolent dictates of the scriptures, the laws of the land, and lead lives consistent with the laws of nature. It is anathema for them to cross the laws of dharma. Such persons, who are a small minority, are said to lead very peaceful lives here and in the hereafter, since they have accumulated good karma.

Rajasic people are the proverbial A-type personalities. Highly energetic and mostly restless, they pursue very down-to-earth policies and follow the goal of artha, or material possessions and power. More wealth and more power give them happiness and the means are less important than the end. Only a few who follow this lifelong pursuit of possessions and power ever succeed in sustaining happiness, leading to the collective unhappiness of this lot.

We then have the third group of people who are dominated by tamas. It is said tamas, because it veils the intellect, makes such people shortsighted. Their happiness lies in sensual gratification. Tasty food, tactile stimulation, attractive visual objects, and captivating sounds dominate their lives. When the senses over a period of time lose their acuity, they have less room to be happy and fall into a state of depression as they get older.

Then there are the spiritual types, the samkhyas, yogis, and vedantins, who relentlessly follow the path of spiritual wisdom and intuitively understand the nature of the ever-present, unchanging nature of their own true Self and reach a state of kaivalya or moksha, which is the ultimate spiritual freedom. In that state, according to yogis, the three gunas reach a state of equilibrium. This yogis call *nirodha*, the cessation of cittavrittis or ceaseless mind activity, a state that the Lord in the Gita calls *gunateeta*, or beyond the dominance of the gunas.

Kārikā 43

The basic nature of experiences, karmic tendencies, and their results

सांसिद्धिकाश्चभावाःप्राकृतिकावैकृताश्चधर्माद्याः ।
दृष्टाःकरणाश्रयिणःकार्याश्रयिणश्चकललाद्याः ॥४३॥

Sāṃsiddhikāścabhāvāḥprākṛtikāvaikṛtāścadharmādyāḥ |
dṛṣṭāḥkaraṇāśrayiṇaḥkāryāśrayiṇaścakalalādyāḥ ||43||

samsiddhikascha—that which is there from the beginning, innate
(lingasarira) prakritikah—a subtle body emerging with the karma bundle created in previous lifetimes
bhavah—tendencies, dispositions

vaikrtika—some karmas produce results immediately but others are held over for a future lifetime

karmashaya—bundle of unripened karmas residing in the subtle body

dharmadhyah—experiences of dharma, knowledge, detachment, sovereignty, as well as their opposites (wrongness, ignorance, attachment, and the absence of power)

karanaashrayanah—a physical body resulting from past karmas

drishtah kaladhyaha ca—body in the embryonic stage depends on karma

// The karmas include acts and experiences both dharmic and nondharmic, including knowledge of the Self or ignorance of it, dispassion toward the worldly or attachment to materiality, attaining supernatural capabilities (siddhis) or servitude to the dictates of prakriti. Every human being can experience dharma, knowledge, detachment, and supernatural powers if one is sattvic. If the person is predominantly tamasic, the opposite of these qualities will prevail. Thus, our situation in life depends on our past karma. //

In the course of life we act variously and accumulate experiences. Some karmas produce results immediately, and some don't; these are held over as karmic bundles (*karmasayas*) that will ripen in a future lifetime. The subtle body holds these karmic experiences as it transmigrates, obtains an embryo, and then develops into a gross physical body.

If the buddhi or intellect is sattvic, it will lead one to go in the path of dharma (righteous action), jnana (knowledge of the Self), vairagya (dispassion), or siddhis (also known as *aisvarya* or *vibhuti*). On the other hand, if the buddhi is highly tamasic, it will go in the path of ignorance, incorrectness, desire, and servitude to the senses and sense objects. Some of these karmas or activities bear fruit immediately, some ripen later in life after a period of time, and some unripened karmas are carried forward as karma bundles into future lifetimes. So, when an entity takes birth as a human being, he or she carries those subtle karmas from previous life cycles. The subtle body with its bundle of karmas first takes human life as *kalaladhya*, or an embryo with a genetic body provided by the parents. These latent karmic impressions are inherent in in the person when they're born, they show up as innate characteristics in the person. During life more activities are done that may be consistent with this innate nature as well as being colored by life circumstances (*vaikruta*). Some past karmas get used up during the present lifetime, and those karmas that are created in the present life but haven't yet ripened will add to the karma bundle for the next lifetime. This is what would happen if a person takes any of the seven paths of dharma,/adharma, ajnana, viraga/aviraga, and aisvarya/anaisvarya. But the one possessing complete knowledge (jnana) of the Self will break free of the chain of samsara and transmigration. So, two things are needed for kaivalya: a sattvic mind, and following the path of jnana, or wisdom, concerning the nature of the Self.

Kārikā 44

Capabilities of a sattvic intellect

धर्मेणगमनमूर्ध्वंगमनमधस्ताद्भवत्यधर्मेण ।
ज्ञानेनचापवर्गोविपर्ययादिष्यतेबन्धः ॥४४॥

Dharmeṇagamanamūrdhvaṃgamanamadhastādbhavatyadharmeṇa |
jñānenacāpavargo viparyayād iṣyate bandhaḥ ||44||

dharmena gamanam urdhvam—good people who are dharmic go upward in their lifetimes, here and hereafter, due to their dharmic activities

adharmena adastath gamanam bhavati—rejecting dharma and embracing adharma takes one downward in future lifetimes

jnanen ca apavargaha—knowledge of purusha takes one to final release and kaivalya, where there are no further births

viparyaya—ignorance about the nature of the Self

bandhashca ishyate—will lead to further in bondage

// With direct knowledge/realization (*jnana*) of the purusha, there is no further transmigration. Those who experience the sattvic qualities of dharma, detachment (*viraga*), and lordship or power (*aisvarya*) will nevertheless remain in bondage without this knowledge, as will those who display the negative qualities of ignorance, attachment, lack of dispassion, and powerlessness. Those who are dharmic advance, but those who are adharmic will regress and remain in bondage and continue to suffer. //

It is important to note that a sattvic buddhi alone is not sufficient for overcoming the three types of duhkha, the goal of Samkhya. Only if a sattvic person is engaged in understanding the nature of the purusha and the nature of the other twenty-four tattvas will that person reach the goal of liberation. Lord Krishna puts it nicely in the Gita (II 50):

Buddhiyukto jahati iha ubhou sukruta dushkruta
Tasmat yogi bhavarjuna yogah karmasu kausalam

A wise person gives up both dharmic and adharmic activities in this world to do only yogic activities. Of all activities, dharmic, adharmic, and yogic, yogic activity is supreme.

Raja yoga is the best of all activities to realize the nature of the Self and reach kaivalya. Buddhi, the intellect, is the most important faculty in a human being. Its direction decides the fate of a person. We have already seen that.

Buddhi in sattvic mode can tread three paths, all of which will lead to less pain and suffering, but only jnana, the path of wisdom about the Self, leads to the permanent cessation of duhkha. Ishvarakrishna describes the results of following the eight different paths a buddhi can take. Buddhi in a sattvic mode can take the path of dharma, which will lead to higher worlds in the future and will uplift one in the present lifetime, with a consequent reduction of duhkha, but it does not help one break out of the vise-like grip of samsara and future births. On the other hand, if the corrupting influence of tamas and rajas, which produces intense craving (*raga*), dominates in the person, it will only lead to lower levels of existence in this life and in the future. The Puranas say these people will wallow in pain in the lower regions of the universe. But through jnana, or wisdom about the nature of the Self, one will get complete release from any involvement in samsaric activity. With the knowledge of the true Self, the person attains cessation of repeated births (*apavarga*). The other paths the buddhi can take are described in the next sloka.

Kārikā 45

The benefits of cultivating dispassion and superior capabilities and the karmic consequences of not doing so

वैराग्यात्प्रकृतिलयःसंसारोभवति राजसाद्१ रागात् ।
ऐश्वर्यादविघातोविपर्ययात्तद्विपर्यासः ॥४५॥

Vairāgyātprakṛtilayaḥsaṃsārobhavati rājasād1 rāgāt |
aiśvaryādavighātoviparyayāttadviparyāsaḥ ||45||

vairagyat prakrutilayah—dispassion and detachment lead to withdrawal and merging into one of the twenty-three aspects or evolutes of prakriti
samsaro bhavathi rajasat ragat—if you don't cultivate detachment, your afflictive emotions will result in transmigration
aishwaryad avighathah—a sattvic mind, through the practice of yoga, can accomplish siddhis (*aisvarya siddhi* and *vibhuti* are synonyms)
viparyayat—without the siddhis
tadvipatyasah—one is directed by the vagaries of the universe and condemned to servitude

// By cultivating detachment and dispassion (*viraga*), one can merge into one of the twenty-three evolutes of prakriti. When afflictive emotions (*raga*) dominate, it will lead to rebirth, whereas detachment without knowledge of the Self, referenced here as *apara*, or lower vairagya, will lead to total withdrawal from the world, a more peaceful life, and merging with a subtle aspect of prakriti, but will not lead to kaivalya. //

The renunciation of the material world (*vairagya*) that arises because of one's sattvic response to the pain we experience in this world is called *apara vairagya*, a detached state of mind. If you cultivate this detached mind, you will be released from this samsaric world for a while and merge into a subtle aspect of prakriti, remaining there without being disturbed by other things until the next life cycle starts. But this state does not afford kaivalya, final liberation, and thus permanent freedom from painful rebirths is not achieved. On the other hand, the person who doesn't cultivate detachment from the world and instead plunges into it headlong will wallow in repeated experiences in samsara.

In his Yoga Sutras (1.19), Patanjali discusses the idea of *videha*, an additional state possible through vairagya in which one's awareness is not confined to the body—a losing of awareness of the physical body—due to apara vairagya coupled with yogic siddhi:

Bhava pratyayo videha prakriti layanam

With an attitude of living forever, yet without knowledge of the atman, the siddha yogi resorts to an out-of-body existence (*videha*) or merging with an aspect of prakriti (*prakriti laya*)

Here is a story from the Puranas:

The great demon (*asura*) Vritra received a boon from God that he would not be destroyed by any weapon. With that mandate, the demon dominated the devas, the heavenly beings. As a result, the whole universe, instead of being governed in an orderly way by the devas, became chaotic under the asuras. The King of the devas, Indra, having lost the fight, hid in a drop of water in the ocean by using his yogic siddhi, or power. This is an example of *prakritilaya*, merging with the subtle aspects of nature. In the Yoga Sutras (1.15, 1.16), Patanjali says,

Drstanusravikavisayavitrsnasyavasikarasamjnavairagyam
Tatparampurusakhyatehgunavaitrsnyam

When one develops vairagya, or dispassion, toward worldly objects but is not inclined to do various Vedic rites leading to different heavens, such vairagya or dispassion is called *vasikara*, or complete self-control. However, the vairagya, or dispassion, toward all three gunas and their manifestations that arise due to the realization of the majesty of the Self, the purusha is superior (*para*).

These two sutras explain the levels of vairagya—the lower, or *apara vairagya*, and the higher, or *para vairagya*. When considering the duhkha that phenomenal life gives, the aspirant naturally wants to get away from the samsaric universe. So, they develop vairagya, dispassion, by systematically working through the four stages leading to control of the senses and mind (*vasikara*). Such people may resort to moving away from worldly life by merging into an evolute of prakriti, like a drop of water as Indra did, or in a kind of out-of-body, "spiritual" existence. Similarly, many people, unable to bear the pain of life on earth, become renunciates (*vairagis* or *bairagis*). But this kind of dispassion does not lead to permanent cessation of samsaric life. Such people will have to be born again, and even though they are able to avoid suffering for a period of time, this is not eternal freedom. On the other hand, the second sutra above describes those yogis who, by direct yogic perception of the Self while in a state of samadhi, develop vairagya toward worldly and otherworldly attractions as a natural consequence. This happens not due to reacting to the perennial pain and sorrow given by mundane life as renunciates (*apara vairagis*) do, but due to knowing the immutable and immortal nature of one's own Self. Such yogis develop a complete dispassion toward whatever prakriti offers. This can be compared to one who is struggling to make both ends meet, who suddenly hits the jackpot and receives millions of dollars. The person will most likely quit the backbreaking job and remain content living off of the bounty. Likewise, the yogi who has realized his own majestic Self will develop minimal interest in his prakritic body-mind.

This same idea can be seen in Ishvarakrishna's Samkhya Karika. He uses two terms—*vairagya* and *jnana*. By *vairagya*, the *apara vairagya* of Patanjali is indicated, and he says such people resort to *prakritilaya*, the same term used by Patanjali to refer to someone submerged in prakriti. On the other hand, someone with a sattvic buddhi who is following the path of knowledge will realize the true nature of the Self and attain the state of *citta vritti nirodha*. Moreover, Patanjali says that when one has an understanding of the purusha, then one develops the highest form of dispassion, *gunavaitrsnyam*, which is detachment from all three gunas.

To summarize:

- The results of the orientation of the buddhi toward dharma will lead to higher worlds.
- Adharma (the opposite of dharma) will take one to intensely painful lower worlds.
- Knowledge, jnana, will lead to final release and liberation (*kaivalya* or *apavarga*).
- Ignorance (*ajnana*) will lead to further bondage consistent with past karmas.
- Cultivating detachment (viraga) will lead to absorption into the universe (*prakritilaya*)
- Attachment to materiality (*aviraga*) and intense afflictive emotions (*raga*) will lead to bondage to samsara.
- Cultivating yogic siddhis (aisvarya) will lead to extraordinary accomplishment.
- Neglect of yogic discipline (*anaisvarya*) will lead to servitude and bondage.

Kārikā 46

The different modes of the buddhi and which are favorable and which are unfavorable for liberation

एषप्रत्ययसर्गोविपर्ययाशक्तितुष्टिसिद्ध्याख्यः ।
गुणवैषम्य१विमर्दात् तस्य च भेदास्तुपञ्चाशत् ॥ ४६॥

Eṣapratyayasargoviparyayāśaktituṣṭisiddhyākhyaḥ |
guṇavaiṣamyaIvimardāttasya ca bhedāstupañcāśat ||46||

esa—now, this
pratyaya, prati-ayam—tendency of the mind, the mood, or the attitude; a form of cittavritti
sarga—the group
viparyaya—wrong understanding of prakriti and purusha
asakti—weakness
tusti—contentment, complacency
siddhi akhyayah—attainment is said to be
gunavaisamyam—imbalance of gunas
vimardat—dominance of one over others, inequality
tasya ca—in the four dimensions of the buddhi disposition (pratyaya)
bhedash tu—their further divisions are
panchasat—said to be fifty

// There are four dimensions/dispositions (*pratyaya*) of the buddhi: wrong perception (*viparyaya pratyaya*), incapacity or inability (*ashakti pratyaya*), contentment (*tusti pratyaya*), and attainment (*siddhi pratyaya*). And because of the imbalance of the gunas, these four can be further divided to make fifty dimensions total. //

Some researchers believe that this and the next few slokas have been added by some later scholars and are not in the original text. They say that these slokas do not appear to be in line with the stream of thought of Ishvarakrishna, and they are not as clearly written as the previous slokas. Nevertheless, some of the old commentators, like sixth-century sage Gaudapada and tenth-century Vedanta philosopher Vacaspatimisra, have commented on this, which means they have accepted these lines as authentic. Sri Krishnamacharya as well included these slokas in his teachings. These slokas provide a very important message.

Here we find a discussion of the mental states of human beings, including those that are favorable for reaching the Samkhya goal of liberation. This is an important contribution concerning the different conditions of the mind. We have already noted that of the eight forms of buddhi, four are sattvic and four others, having the opposite characteristics, are said to be tamasic.

- dharma/adharma
- vairagya/avairagya
- aisvarya/anaisvarya
- jnana/ajnana

These tendencies of the mind are related to the eight modes of the buddhi, or intellect. The first tendency is knowledge (*jnana*) or its opposite, ignorance (*ajnana*) and is termed viparyaya here. Then there is weakness, harm, or injury to the organs of causation (*karanas*), of which there are thirteen types (enumerated in a later sloka). The author then explains the nature of the two remaining mental tendencies as contentment or complacency (*tushti*) and accomplishment (*siddhi*). In these, the positive/negative tendencies toward dharma/adharma, vairagya/avairagya, aisvarya/anaisvarya, and ajnana fall under the categories of wrong perception (*viparyaya*) with respect to understanding the real nature of the Self, incapacity or infirmity (*ashakti*), or contentment (*tushti*). Furthermore, it can be said that wrong perception includes adharma and ajnana, two tamasic modes of the buddhi. Attachment (*avairagya*) and complete servitude to prakriti or to sense objects and powerlessness (*anaisvarya*) come under the category of *ashakti*, infirmity. Contentment includes forms of detachment (*vairagya*), dharma, and superior powers (*aisvarya*), the three sattvic modes of the buddhi. The last lone form of the buddhi, knowledge (*jnana*), falls under the category of siddhi, or accomplishment. Siddhi is the only mental mode or pratyaya for reaching kaivalya according to Samkhya.

Kārikā 47

Further elaboration of the four tendencies of the mind

पञ्चविपर्ययभेदाभवन्त्यशक्तेश्चकरणवैकल्यात् ।
अष्टाविंशतिभेदास्तुष्टिर्नवधाष्टधासिद्धिः ॥ ४७॥

Pañcaviparyayabhedābhavantyaśakteścakaraṇavaikalyāt |
aṣṭāviṃśatibhedāstuṣṭirnavadhāṣṭadhāsiddhiḥ ||47||

viparyaya bhedah—the wrong knowledge (*viparyaya*) categories
pancha bhavanti—are five in number
asakti ca—weakness or infirmity
karana vaikalyat—due to the degradation of instruments of action, perception, and internal organs
ashta vimsati bhedah—are twenty-eight different types
tushti—contentment, complacency
navadha—is of nine varieties
siddhih—accomplishment
ashtadha—is of eight types

// The four tendencies of the mind (*pratyayas*) are subdivided into fifty types as follows: incorrect knowledge (*viparyaya*) is of five types; infirmity (*asakti*) is of twenty-eight types; contentment (*tushti*) is of nine types; and accomplishment (*siddhi*) is of eight types, making in all fifty varieties of pratyaya, or mental modes. //

Patanjali lists five groups of cittavritties, or activities of the citta or brain. Ishvarakrishna categorizes the mental modes into four groups and uses the term *pratyaya* to indicate these mental modes. Patanjali further divide the cittavritties into two groups: those that are favorable (*aklishta*) and those that are unfavorable (*klishta*). Favorable vritties are those yogic activities that would lead the person toward kaivalya through *citta vritti nirodha*, or stopping all mental activites. Of Ishvarakrishna's four pratyayas, the most useful group for attaining kaivalya is the siddhi pratyaya. These four are further refined to make a total of fifty pratyayas.

Kārikā 48

Types of wrong understanding

भेदस्तमसोऽष्टविधोमोहस्य च दशविधोमहामोहः ।
तामिस्रोऽष्टादशधातथाभवत्यन्धतामिस्रः ॥४८॥

Bhedastamaso'ṣṭavidhomohasya ca daśavidhomahāmohaḥ |
tāmisro'ṣṭādaśadhātathābhavatyandhatāmisraḥ ||48||

tamasah—ignorance (or *avidya*)
bhedah—divisions are
ashtavidhau—eight types
mohasya—of delusion (*moha*) or pride (*asmita*)
ca—also (eight types)
mahamoha—great delusion (*mahamoha*) is of ten types (*raga dasavidhah*)
tamisrah—hatred, anger, a division of hell (*tamisra*) or aversion (*dvesha*, one of the five poisons)

ashtadasada—is of eighteen types
tatha—likewise of eighteen types
bhavanti—are there
andhatamisrah—deep darkness, annihilation (*andhatamisra*), fear (*abhinivesha*)

// The types of incorrect knowing (*viparyaya*) according to Samkhya are said to be five. They are ignorance (*tamas*), and this itself is subdivided into eight types: delusion (*moha*), also of eight types; great delusion (*mahamoha*), of ten types; darkness (*tamisra*), said to be of eighteen types; and deep darkness of the mind (*andhatamisra*), also of eighteen types. //

The ways of incorrect knowing (*viparyaya*) are related to the *kleshas* as delineated by Patanjali in the Yoga Sutras and as authored by commentators like Vacaspatimisra. These kleshas are further elaborated into sixty-two variants. The *viparyaya*, or wrong understanding, is divided into five, which are *tamas*, *moha*, *mahamoha*, *tamisra*, and *andhatamisra*. Many scholars relate these viparyayas of Samkhya to the pain (the five *kleshas*) mentioned in Yoga philosophy. Tamas here is ignorance (*avidya*); *moha*, or delusion, would be to consider that the intellect has consciousness; *mahamoha*, is intense attachment, desire, or passion; *tamisra*, or darkness, would be hatred; and *andhatamisra* would be fear or more specifically, a fear of death.

Yoga students may find this discussion in Samkhya very helpful in understanding the five afflictions of the mind (*pancha kleshas*) or root obstacles of Kriya Yoga.

Tamas, the first viparyaya of samkhyas, or ignorance (*avidya*) is of eight types. What are they? To consider the buddhi as the Self; to think of the ahamkara, the ego, as the Self; to regard the mulaprakriti of the three gunas as the Self, without any knowledge of the pure consciousness; and to consider the five subtle tanmatras as the Self. These are the eight types of obscurations in the group categorized as Samkhya's tamas or Patanjali's avidya. This grouping is called tamas (name given by samkhyas) and is known as *avidya klesha*, the obscuration of ignorance, by yogis.

Considering the five tanmatras' evolutes of earth, water, fire, air, and space as the Self is also ignorance. So is considering the three aspects of the mind (the buddhi, manas, and ahamkara) as the Self. As Patanjali says in the Yoga Sutras (11.5),

Anitya, asuchi, duhkha anatamsu, nitya, suchi, sukha atma khyatiravidya|

Considering what is impermanent as eternal, what is unwholesome or unclean as good, what is painful as happiness, and above all considering the temporary nonself as the immortal Self is called *avidya*, or absolute ignorance.

Clearly, then, the tendency of human beings to consider the physical body as the true Self is ignorance and therefore tamasic. So to consider the physical body, which is comprised of the five elements—the default (mis)understanding of the Self by almost the entire human race—is a classic case of ignorance.

The next klesha is *moha*, or pride, or Patanjali's asmita. This can be divided into eight types. Some yogis, due to their extraordinary siddhis, might consider the eight forms of divine knowledge, called the *ashtama siddhis*,* as eternal and thus falsely assume themselves to be immortal. This form of pride is delusion (*moha*).

Once *avidya*, ignorance, is well-established in a person, that person will tend to divide objects into favorable and unfavorable and get overly attached to favorable objects. This is called *raga*,

*1) *Aṇimā*, the ability to reduce one's body to the size of an atom; 2) *Mahimā*, the ability to expand one's body to an infinitely large size; 3) *Laghimā*, the ability to become weightless, or lighter than air; 4) *Garimā*, the ability to become heavy or dense; 5) *Prāpti*, the ability to realize whatever one desires; 6) *Prākāmya*, the ability to access any place in the world; 7) *Īśitva*, the ability to control all material elements or natural forces; and 8) *Vaśitva*, the ability to influence anyone.

intense attachment, by yogis, and *mahamoha*, or massive delusion, by samkhyas. Objects are known only as sensations, and attachment to these sensations are produced. Some people get attached to sound, like getting fixated on rock music or constantly engaging in small talk. Others get attached to tasty gourmet food. There are some who get addicted to tactile sensations, whether produced by other human beings, pets, or other objects. Sensations such as these were considered worldly, otherworldly, or even divine in past ages. Patanjali describes certain siddhis that he calls *divyam srotram*, "divine sounds." Some people get completely attached to these extraordinary sensations, and here Ishvarakrishna calls them *mahamoha*, "great delusion." Since there are five sensations that can be produced by worldly objects and five divine sensations, these afflictions are said to be ten in number.

The next form of ignorance is called misery (*tamisra*) by samkhyas, or hatred (*dvesha*) by Patanjali. This is said to be of eighteen types. It includes the negativity one feels from not getting what one wants, as in the previous kleshas. When a person desires any of the ten sensations or the eight siddhis mentioned earlier and fails to get them, then the pain of this failure is called *tamisra*, misery, or *dvesha*, hatred. Not getting sensations like tactile pleasure or the inability to hear subtle divine sounds, or a yogi not attaining siddhis are examples of this. So, this lack of fulfillment of the eighteen types is considered to be eighteen types of misery.

The next form of incorrect knowing is called deep darkness, or *andhatamisra*, by samkhyas, and fear of losing or even death, or *abhinivesha*, by yogis. In the previous discussion, one can develop hatred or aversion (*dvesha*) when one does not get any of the eighteen things one desires. And those who already have any of the ten sensations or the eight siddhis, or even some of them, fear losing them. Not getting what one wants leaves a bad feeling, a *dvesha*. And fear of losing what is already obtained is another cause of suffering. These forms of ignorance, attachment, and so forth can be eradicated only by realizing the nature of the true Self, the purusha. These last two viparyayas or kleshas can be classified as *tapa*, or restlessness. The misery of not getting what one wants is *tamisra*. And those who have obtained them fear losing them and that would be *andhatamisra*.

Kārikā 49

The twenty-eight afflictions

एकादशेन्द्रियवधाःसहबुद्धिवधैरशक्तिरुद्दिष्टा ।
सप्तदशवधाबुद्धेर्विपर्ययात्तुष्टिसिद्धीनाम् ॥४९॥

Ekādaśendriyavadhāḥsahabuddhivadhairaśaktiruddiṣṭā |
saptadaśavadhābuddherviparyayāttuṣṭisiddhīnām ||49||

ekadasaindriya—of the eleven sense organs
vadhah—infirmities, afflictions
buddhivadhaihsaha—along with the infirmity of the buddhi
uddhishta—are considered
asakti—infirmity
tushti—contentment
siddhi—accomplishment
viparyayat—being absent
saptadasa—seventeen
vadhah—affliction or infirmities

// The afflictions number twenty-eight. They include the afflictions of the ten sense organs (*indriyas*) along with that of the intellect (*buddhi*). The absence of the nine forms of contentment (*tushti*) and the eight accomplishments (*siddhis*) constitute an additional seventeen infirmities, for a total of twenty-eight infirmities (*asaktis*). //

Infirmities of the body produce their own types of weakness that can prevent one from reaching the goal of liberation according to Ishvarakrishna. Defects of any one or more of the ten sense organs leads to this type of affliction. Defects of the eyes could prevent one from seeing objects. Defective hearing could prevent one from listening to the Vedas and thus the person would be unable to study the Vedas, as in ancient times the Vedas were only heard and not written. Thus in times past, loss of hearing was considered a weakness that could prevent the aspirant from acquiring the required knowledge. Similarly, defects of the organs of action (*karmendriyas*) like the legs, arms, and so forth can create difficulties, and so Ishvarakrishna describes these defects as creating obstacles to realization. Furthermore, even if the sense organs are in good condition, if the buddhi, or intellect, is defective, these sense organs cannot be properly used to acquire knowledge of the Self. Thus there are eleven weaknesses due to infirmities of the body and mind.

In addition, a lack of *tushti*, or contentment (there are nine of these, described in the next sloka), and the failure to realize the eight siddhis or the means of attaining kaivalya can add to disturbances of the buddhi . . . Thus there are twenty-eight different types of infirmities—ten due to defects in the physical sense organs, one due to a defect of the intellect, nine due to nonattainment of contentment, and eight due to the nonattainment of the eight siddhis.

Kārikā 50

The nine types of contentment or complacency

आध्यात्मिकाश्चतस्त्रः प्रकृत्युपादानकालभागयाख्याः।
बाह्याविषयोपरमाच्चपञ्चनवतुष्टयोऽभिमताः ॥५०॥

Adhyātmikāścatasraḥprakṛtyupādānakālabhāgyākhyāḥ |
bāhyāviṣayoparamāccapañcanavatuṣṭayo'bhimatāḥ ||50||

adhyatmikyah—concerning ourselves internally
catasrah—of four types
prakriti—nature
upadana—means
kala—time
bhagya—luck
vishaya uparamat bahya panca—developing dispassion toward objects of the five senses giving pleasure through touch, taste, sound, sight, or smell
tushtayah—contentment or complacency
prakrtitusti—being complacent that nature in due course will bring about release, as in "I know what is to be known, but I am not going to do anything, I am going to allow prakriti to do everything."
nava—nine
abhimatah—are determined
upadana—to follow a regimen, to follow an order as directed by one or the other
kala—in the course of time everything will happen, kaivalya will have to happen
bhagya—luck

// There are nine types of satisfaction/complacency (*tushti*)—four internal, related to the satisfaction derived from prakriti, from material aspects, complacently believing that time and luck will rectify everything; and five external, which is nonattachment to the five sense objects. By developing detachment (*vairagya*) toward the five external sense objects that relate to the material world, one remains in a state of contentment wrongly thinking this vairagya will deliver. //

This sloka introduces the nine types of contentment or complacency; both are called *tushti*. Contentment is a state of desirelessness or dispassion in which one experiences a sense of peaceful pleasure, whereas complacency is equated with a sense of smug self-satisfaction.

Many systems in the olden days preached dispassion or vairagya as a means of reducing pain and getting a certain peace of mind. Many would take to a life of self-negation without proactively trying to understand the nature of the Self. Such people are content that they have done what is to be done. This contentment would make them complacent.

Vairagya, detachment, is derived from the word *viraga*, which combines *raga*, "passionate attachment," with the prefix *vi*, meaning "without." *Raga* is a word most yogis are familiar with, as it is considered a klesha, a pain-creator. Raga implies an intense attachment, almost like glue—it's very difficult to tear away from an object that one is glued to. That is why detachment (*vairagya*) is an attitude of dispassion that the yogi must practice. Ordinary mortals, or the beginning yogi, along with practicing asanas, should consciously practice vairagya and develop worldly detachment (*viraga bhava*) toward material objects. On the other hand, the evolved sattvic yogi or born yogi who can easily get into a state of samadhi must be very careful not to become distracted by the allure of yogic accomplishments or siddhis, which is why the word *complacency* is also offered here, meaning the tendency to rest on one's laurels in a state of smug self-satisfaction. Yoga practitioners who have a tamasic disposition when starting yoga practice will likely find themselves overly attached to sense objects, whereas rajasic beginners will find power and possessions alluring. Sattvic beginners are far more inclined to follow dharma and stick to yogic precepts.

The yoga practitioner has to constantly be vigilant concerning detachment, or vairagya. Vairagya can be *para vairagya*, or higher vairagya, and *apara vairagya*, or lower vairagya. Lower vairagya is something everyone can relate to and observe as part of their yoga practice. You start with an object of one of the senses and try to overcome your attachment to that object. For example, if I am addicted to coffee, I may try to make a conscious effort to get over my dependence on coffee. By slowly reducing the amount and frequency of coffee breaks, I may be able to overcome my addiction to coffee. Once I am able to overcome my attachment to coffee, I may attempt to identify other objects that enslave me through my sense of taste. Through conscious effort over a period of time, I will be able to have control over what I eat and thus bring one of my senses under control. This is the first stage. Once I am able to slowly bring my tongue under control, then the first stage of apara vairagya takes place. I have cultivated detachment, but am still only at the first stage.

If I maintain this dispassionate state for some time and it develops into a habit, a samskara, I will experience a sense of well-being and develop a healthy disposition toward renunciation. Enthused, I may attempt to gradually bring the other senses under control. When I am able to completely control all five senses and wean myself away from their slavish tendency to attach to objects, I will have reached the second stage of apara vairagya.

Now my attachment to objects only remains in a subdued state in my mind, the eleventh sense faculty (*indriya*), and does not manifest through my senses. This stage is called *ekendriya samnja*, "only in mind."

Then we come to the fourth state of apara vairagya, which Patanjali calls *vasikara samjna vairagya*, "total vairagya." In this state the yogi develops complete detachment mentally to outer world experiences, including from the sensual pleasures the world offers.

Then there are yogis who have an inborn samadhi capability or who have acquired it through diligent yoga practice. These outstanding individuals may, nevertheless, develop attachments to various heavens mentioned in the scriptures or to various siddhis and spend a lifetime in pursuit of such accomplishments. Developing dispassion toward heavenly bliss or jaw-dropping yogic siddhis is the fourth stage of vairagya, called *vasikara vairagya*, in which even the mind ceases to become attached to objects. Yogis who are able to master this final stage of vairagya may end up existing in an out-of-body state or merge with some subtle aspect of prakriti, yet will fall short of the mental state required to attain the final goal of kaivalya. This is a mental state of complacency or satisfaction, an attitude of "rolling with the punches."

There are four internal forms of complacency and five external forms. The first internal form of complacency is based on a kind of laziness and is called *prakriti tushti*. Even after acquiring secondhand knowledge of the Self, one makes no further effort to experience it directly through appropriate means, such as by practicing Raja Yoga. For example, say I have heard about the nature of prakriti and purusha, and I believe that somehow purusha realization will come about, so I make no further effort.

A second form of internal complacency is called *upadana*, or paying attention only to the external means of achieving kaivalya. Having understood that the universe is full of duhkha, I decide to become a renunciate. Yet I make no real attempt to get to know the atman by practicing internal yoga, and instead

I follow the niyamas of a recluse by wearing orange robes, leaving home and becoming a nomad, and displaying all the external signs of a yogi, such as carrying a staff, shaving my head (or the opposite, growing long matted hair). The belief that merely displaying the outer signs of being a sanyasin and following the niyamas and rituals and wearing external signs will somehow get me to kaivalya is the second internal complacency.

Next is the inner complacency tushti that kaivalya will happen in due course. "Time will solve all problems" is the attitude. With this tushti the person remains content that liberation will somehow come in time and so they just wait it out.

Then there is the fourth form of inner complacency, the attitude that internal contentment depends on luck. If I am lucky, I will win the lottery and spend time and money on more lottery tickets. In the same vein, this attitude says I will get kaivalya because one day I will hit the spiritual jackpot.

External complacency tushtis are of five types. Once the aspirant encounters bookish knowledge of the atman and prakriti, he or she becomes complacent about activities that require still more to be done. Different scholars explain this differently. One approach involves looking at the duhkha the external world produces and deciding to simply put up with it—in effect, to just grin and bear it. For example, upon discovering that getting a job in the "real world" and earning a livelihood is strenuous, you stop working to earn money and decide to live in poverty. Then comes another form of external complacency, when even if you do earn and manage to save, protecting your assets is duhkha. A third form comes when once you save and start using your money, it becomes depleted, and that too is a source of suffering. A fourth form is illustrated by loss due to theft or taxes, another form of duhkha. Finally, a fifth form involves acquiring money and things, which usually causes injury to other beings, so the attitude is I'll just eschew all efforts to live in the "real world" and become a renunciate.

Some scholars refer to the five senses and develop dispassion toward the objects of the five senses as they do not produce permanent satisfaction and require more and more effort to provide the same satisfaction. These nine pratyayas, called *tushti pratyaya*, do not lead to the ultimate goal of kaivalya state, a state in which the three types of duhkha are permanently and definitively removed. These tushti pratyayas are impediments to achieving the goal of liberation. Why so? One becomes complacent and does not put the necessary efforts to achieve kaivalya. The kaivalya aspirant wanting duhkha to go away forever and definitively will have to be proactive by practicing wholesome yoga.

Kārikā 51

The eight factors that bring siddhis/success

ऊहः शब्दोऽध्ययनंदुःखविघातास्त्रयःसुहृत्प्राप्तिः ।
दानं च सिद्धयोऽष्टौ२ सिद्धेःपूर्वोऽङ्कुशस्त्रिविधः ॥५१॥

ūhaḥśabdo>dhyayanaṃduḥkhavighātāstrayaḥsuhṛtprāptiḥ |
dānaṃ ca siddhayo'ṣṭausiddhe ḥpūrvo'ṅkuśastrividhaḥ ||51||

uhah—to have all the information, then come to a conclusion through deep contemplation and inference
shabdh—oral instruction
dhuhkha vighatah trayah—removal or suppression of the three sources of suffering

suhrit prapti—to consult a like-minded person who has a better understanding, after first studying by oneself

danam—offering, repaying one's teacher's kindness

siddhayoshtau—eight avenues of achieving the ultimate goal

siddhe purvonkushah—impediments to attaining the goal

trividhah—three types of obstacles: incorrect knowledge (*viparyaya*), incapacity (*asakti*), and contentment (*tushti*)

Ankusah—impediments, restraints

There are eight methods or favorable mental tendencies (*pratyayas*) needed to achieve the ultimate goal: reasoning/inference (*uhah*), oral instruction (*sabda*), study (*adhyayana*), suppression/ reduction of the three forms of suffering (*duhkhavighatah*), acquisition of like-minded knowledgeable friends (*suhrtprapti*), and making offerings (*dana*) to your esteemed teacher.

The eight attainments necessary for overcoming the three forms of suffering and accomplishing the ultimate Samkhya goal of liberation are:

1. **Reasoning (*uhah*):** This means to have all the information and then come to a conclusion oneself. The whole idea is that nobody can achieve kaivalya for us, nor will it happen in due course. Ultimately each of us has to find and move in our own path to liberation.

2. **Oral instruction (*sabda*):** Oral instruction from a qualified teacher is helpful or even necessary for achieving the ultimate goal.

3. **Study (*adhyayana*):** Along with the words of the teacher, engage in your own study.

4–6. **Suppressing the three forms of suffering (*duhkhavighatah*):** When the three forms of suffering—that which is self-induced (*adhyatmika*), that which is caused by other beings (*adhibhautika*), and that which is caused by forces of nature (*adhidaivika*)—manifest, then one should take whatever steps possible, such as the path of detachment (*vairagya*), to reduce the forms of suffering so that they do not distract from the ultimate goal.

7. **Seek good company (*suhrtprapti*):** Once you've begun studying yourself, consult others who have a better understanding, or join a proper sangha.

8. **Making offerings, or repaying the teacher's kindness (*dana*):** If you find a qualified person with the knowledge to impart the true teachings, make a financial offering to him or her and learn. Don't hesitate.

There are four tendencies of the mind, or *pratyayas*: incorrect knowing (*viparyaya*), incapacity or impairment (*asakti*), contentment or complacency (*tushti*), and accomplishment (*siddhi*). Of these four, the first three are impediments, and only accomplishment, siddhi, is helpful for the complete and permanent removal of duhkha. In a similar vein, Patanjali, in his Yoga Sutras, divides the cittavrittis into unfavorable and favorable. Just as the reasoning (*uhah*) group is considered favorable by samkhyas, Patanjali considers yogic activities and vrittis as equally favorable for attaining kaivalya, and all nonyogic activities as being not very helpful in reaching the ultimate goal.

As we know from the previous sloka, the term *pratyaya* refers to a person's basic mental tendencies or contents of the mind. This word appears throughout Patanjali's Yoga Sutras.* The word *pratyaya* (or *pratyayam*) consists of the root syllables *prati*

*Yoga Sutras 1.10, 1.18, 1.19, 2.20, 3.2, 3.12, 3.17, 3.19, 3.35, and 4.27

plus *ayam* (or *ayam prati pratyayam*). While *prati* has different shades of meaning, here it means "to" or "toward," while *ayam* is "this." Since this word is used in the context of the mind, the citta, many scholars refer to pratyaya as one's mental state at any given moment. Some scholars relate pratyaya to the cittavrittis.

In Yoga Sutra 2.20, which describes the Self, purusha, Patanjali says,

Draṣṭā dṛśimātraḥ śuddho'pi pratyayānupaśyaḥ

The seer (*drashta*) has only one function—that of witnessing. It is pure in that it does not have any of the changing qualities of prakriti, which are the three gunas. Even so, it is constrained to simply be overseeing the manifest activities of the citta, which are the *cittavritties or pratyaya*.

We know that consciousness continuously observes the cittavrittis. According to Patanjali, these innumerable cittavrittis fall into five groups. A perhaps more detailed interpretation of Patanjali's description of the pratyayas can be found in Samkhya, especially since Samkhya is a sibling philosophy of Yoga, and both are said to derive their inspiration from the Vedas. Samkhya is a thorough and unique evidence-based philosophical system, and Yoga further develops on the Samkhya framework to accomplish the goal of liberation. So, let's see what Samkhya has to say about the pratyayas.

Samkhya's classification of pratyayas directs us to those favorable pratyayas that help us understand the twenty-five tattvas, especially the all-important purusha, which is the sole means of overcoming the three types of duhkha referred to by both yogis and samkhyas. These are the eight pratyayas that bring siddhis, what are called *siddhi pratyayas*, or those mental states conducive to leading one to kaivalya, or freedom from duhkha, definitively and forever.

Yogis are no doubt familiar with the concept of siddhi, and

Patanjali expounds on the subject in his Yoga Sutras. The mother of all siddhis, of course, is direct perception of the unwavering consciousness that is the purusha, the Self, by the buddhi of an aspirant who is in a state of samadhi. Here Ishvarakrishna explains the eight mental states that lead to this state of kaivalya, as well as the precise state of the mind when one has achieved that state of liberation.

The first helpful state is *uhah*, yogic mental effort through reasoning. This includes the whole group of internal practices that yogis are familiar with. Once an aspirant gets all the information, he or she must thoroughly analyze and internalize it. There is the example of Bhrugu, the son of Varuna, a story found in the Taittiriya Upanishad that contains the Pancha Kosha *vidya* that many yogis are familiar with. Bhrugu, who came to learn about Brahman, the ultimate reality, sought his father's help to completely understand it, know it, and directly experience it. The father gives a definition of Brahman as the one from which everything is created, by which everything is sustained, and finally into which everything merges. This is the path of oral instruction through hearing, *sabda*. Here the father, Varuna, acted truly as an *acharya*, one who shows the path, rather than simply carrying his son who is his disciple on his shoulders. The well-known story is that by following this teaching, Bhrugu realizes the true nature of Brahman by rejecting the five layers, or *koshas*, of the physical body as not being the true Self. Thus the individual yogic mental effort Bhrugu exerted, called *uhah*, is absolutely an important step needed to reach the ultimate state of kaivalya, while oral instruction, *sabda*, further increased his understanding. These philosophies—Yoga, Samkhya, Vedanta—all require not only reading but deep contemplation so that one is convinced that it is right.

Study (*adhyayana*) of texts such as the Vedas, especially the philosophical portions like the Upanishads and texts like Samkhya, is a third requirement. *Dana* means making offerings, usually financial, to your guru (also known as *gurudakshina*), a fourth requirement. *Suhrtprapti* means the acquisition of correct Samkhya knowledge obtained from like-minded and knowledgeable friends, making for the fifth requirement. Finally, *duhkhavighatah* refers to eradication/significant reduction of the three forms of suffering: inherent suffering, that caused by other creatures, and that caused by natural factors. These consist of the favorable pratyayas or mental states for the one who is looking for a way to overcome the three types of perennial suffering that samkhyas, yogis, and vedantis urge us to permanently and definitively eradicate within this very lifetime. Added together (with *duhkhavighatah* comprising three of the eight forms), these make for a total of eight forms of siddhi pratyaya.

The remaining twenty-eight pratyayas are termed *asakti*, impairment or weakness of the sense faculties, which also affects state of mind. If the mind is not in one of nine states of contentment or complacency (*tushti*) or eight states of sidhhi as described above, it is considered impaired. So, in all we have forty-two states of mind—five *viparyayas* (faulty understanding), twenty-eight *asaktis* (infirmities), and nine *tushtis* (contentments or complacencies), all of which are considered unfavorable states of mind and therefore impediments (ankusa) for the development of the pratyayas that are favorable for removing duhkha, the siddhi pratyayas.

As mentioned earlier, the term *pratyaya* is repeatedly found in Patanjali's Yoga Sutras (2.20). He defines purusha as the seer who merely witnesses and is untarnished by the presence of any of the three gunas:

द्रष्टा दृशिमात्रः शुद्धोपि प्रत्ययानुपश्यः

Draṣṭā dṛśimātraḥ śuddhopi pratyayānupaśyaḥ

The indwelling consciousness called *drashta*, or seer, observes the cittavrittis, the manifest activities of the mind, or citta.

It is pure, uncontaminated by the three gunas of prakriti. It is limited to simply overseeing the pratyayas, or the mental activities.

The purusha always sees the object in the form of a pratyaya or mental state. We mistakenly consider the physical person as the Self and outside things as objects. But according to Patanjali, the subject is not the body-mind complex—it is the unchanging consciousness called *purusha*. The eight siddhi pratyayas are what are necessary for obtaining kaivalya from the viewpoint of both samkhyas and yogis. The other forty-two pratyayas, made up of five *viparyayas* (incorrect understanding), nine *tushtis* (complacencies), and twenty-eight *asaktis* (infirmities) are impediments, especially for spiritual pursuits, or even, quite frankly, for mundane pursuits.

Kārikā 52

Two factors necessary for rebirth

न विनाभावैर्लिङ्गं न विनालिङ्गेनभावनिर्वृत्तिः ।
लिङ्गाख्योभावाख्यस्तस्माद्विविधाःप्रवर्ततेसर्गः ॥५२॥

Navinābhāvairliṅgaṃnavināliṅgenabhāvanirvṛttiḥ |
liṅgākhyobhāvākhyastasmāddvividhāḥpravartatesargaḥ ||52||

na vina bhavairlingam na vina lingena bhava nivritti—without the subtle body, the effects of karma cannot take place
lingakhya—the elemental
bhavakhya—the dispositions

pravartate dvividham—proceed into two streams
sargah—creation of the subtle body and physical body.

// Two things that are necessary for transmigration. Without experiences, feelings, and emotions (*bhava*), as well as karma that has not yet ripened, the subtle body will not be able to function, as there is no motivation or driving force for it to do so. It becomes stale, and there is no impulse forward. Hence ignorance and unripened karma push you forward to the next rebirth. //

Without the subtle body, the effects of karma cannot take place. Therefore, the subtle body source (*linga*) and the emotional dispositions (*bhavakhya*) proceed in two streams to create the subtle body and the physical body. The subtle body is created first, and the physical body is then created because of the various emotional dispositions that have arisen as a result of experiences and unripened karma. We need a subtle body to hold the bhavas, which then create a physical body.

Simply put, there are two streams in prakritic creation: the subjective stream, which gives the subtle body, and the objective stream, which consists of the elements, or *bhutas*. The bhutas themselves emanate from the tanmatras to provide objects to experience. The subtle body, or *linga*, acquires the elements and in this way acquires a physical body.

Kārikā 53

Here a different aspect of creation is described

अष्टविकल्पोदैवस्तइर्यग्योनश्चपञ्चधाभवति ।
मानुष्यश्चैकविधःसमासतोभौतिकःसर्गः ॥५३॥

aṣṭavikalpodaivastairyagyonaścapañcadhābhavati |
mānuṣyaścaikavidhaḥsamāsatobhautikaḥsargaḥ ||53||

ashtavikalpah—they can be divided into eight groups
daiva—celestial beings
tiryakyonasca—animals
pancadabhavathi—five groups are there
manushya ca ekavidhah—the human race is only one
bhautikah—creatures
sargah—are these as mentioned

//Here the creation of various entities is described. First, there are the devas, or celestial beings. Among the devas there are different classes or groups that encompass divine beings such as Brahma, the Vedic deity Prajapati, the moon goddess Soumya, Indra, as well as the gandharvas, yakshas, rakshasas, and demons. There are five groups of animals, but human beings are only of one kind. //

***Question*:** What are we yoga practitioners trying to do by studying Samkhya? How does yoga help us achieve the goal of Samkhya?
***Answer*:** If you find that Samkhya alone is not sufficient to meet your desire to advance spiritually and achieve kaivalya, then you need to get the help of Yoga. Yoga is much more than mere physical practices; it provides the necessary theoretical foundation in a way that is accessible for most all aspirants. Yoga begins by spelling out the path for achieving liberation, a matter addressed by Vedanta as well. What it says is that if your desire for *moksha* is intense, then you'll be focused on it all the time, and that alone is sufficient to take you to your goal. This kind of intense focus is like the effort made by someone who is drowning and

gasping to hang on to dear life. You're not merely musing, *Oh, how I wish I could be a yogi . . .* You're contemplating the principles and the prakritic tattvas, and meditating on the nature of the Self. If you are able to do this easily, then you're a born yogi. Such a person doesn't need to do Ashtanga or Hatha yoga, as they can get into samadhi without practicing asanas. If your understanding of the basic principles is solid, then your mind will not be distracted by anything else. So, find out what works for you. If you think your understanding is strong enough, then you can straightaway proceed on the path. On the other hand, if you're convinced about the verity of the underlying principles but feel you're still falling short of your goal, then yogic practices such as following the yamas and niyamas and practicing asana and pranayama will be helpful. In fact, in Vedanta they say there's nothing wrong in making use of yoga practices, but for people of a certain aptitude it is simply not necessary. So don't tell an experienced vedantin or samkhya that they must do vrischikasana regularly or sit down and meditate and get into samadhi—it's not necessary for them.

So here in Samkhya the emphasis is more on understanding the elements of the universe, the nature of one's Self, and the goal of human birth, which is to overcome the pain and sorrow inherent in life. Yoga too emphasizes this understanding, but not everyone has the same capacity for achieving samadhi, hence the different (but related) methods of Samkhya and Yoga. So if you do not have the capacity to easily get into samadhi, start with Kriya yoga and then proceed to Ashtanga yoga. Yoga makes it possible for anyone, even those at the beginner level, to succeed. Suppose you are sixty years old, then yoga asanas may be difficult. In that case start with Kriya yoga to reduce the *kleshas*. As we have seen thus far, reducing the kleshas that cause duhkha is one of the ways of doing this, which is what you're doing when you practice Kriya yoga. So you have to discover what yoga practices will be appropriate for you at whatever stage or age you're at. Not everyone should sit down and practice asana and pranayama. Other methods are available, so find out what's appropriate for you, or maybe your teacher will be able to guide you on the appropriate path, as Sri Krishnamacharya would do for his students.

Kārikā 54

The gunas and their dominance in the three regions of the universe

ऊर्ध्वंसत्त्वविशालस्तमोविशालश्चमूलतःसर्गः ।
मध्येरजोविशालोब्रह्मादिस्तम्बपर्यन्तः ॥५४॥

Urdhvaṃsattvaviśālastamoviśālaścamūlataḥsargaḥ |
madhyerajoviśālobrahmādistambaparyantaḥ ||54||

urdhvam—upward or upper regions, the heavens
sattva vishaalah—is dominated by sattva
sargah mulatah tamovishala—tamas dominates the nether region
madhyarajovishalah—in the middle region rajas dominates
brahmadi—the topmost heaven; brahma is sattvic entity
stambha—blade or bunch of grass is tamasic
paryantam—up to that, this rule applies to all of them

// Sattva dominates the upper regions and that is why they say heaven is above us. Tamas dominates the lower region, and

in the middle region rajas dominates. *Brahmadi* here refers to *caturmukha brahma*, that is, the topmost heaven. Such is creation, ranging from a lowly clump of grass, which is tamasic, to brahma, who is sattvic. //

***Question*:** Why is Samkhya considered a Vedic philosophy when it is supposedly atheistic?

***Answer*:** It is a Vedic philosophy, so it is part of Vedas. There are six different philosophies that subscribe to the Vedas. There are disagreements among them, but even as they may disagree, just as children of the same family disagree but belong to the same family, they nevertheless work against a common adversary: duhkha. As far as being atheistic, Samkhya does not say God does not exist, therefore you cannot say it is atheistic. The study of the concept of the mind (*astikadarshana*) in the Upanishads and the concept of theism are two different things. Samkhya is a philosophy concerning the study of the mind and the true Self. *Astikadarshana* refers to those philosophies that follow the Vedas (*astika* implies that all that you want to know is in the Vedas). There are many other philosophies that discuss the nature of God, but in Samkhya we study the nature of the mind and the Self. The word *astika* means one who believes in the Vedas. Many faiths belive in God but are not considered "astika," as such faiths do not believe in the Vedas.

Kārikā 55

Duhkha, or the pain of repeated rebirths

तत्रजरामरणकृतंदुःखंप्राप्नोतिचेतनःपुरुषः ।
लिङ्गस्याविनिवृत्तेस्तस्माद्दुःखंस्वभावेन ॥५५॥

tatrajarāmaraṇakṛtaṃduḥkhaṃprāpnoticetanaḥpuruṣaḥ |
liṅgasyāvinivṛttestasmādduḥkhaṃsvabhāvena ||55||

tatra—in this creation
jara marana krutam—of old age and death
duhkham—suffering, fear
purusah—individual entity
lingasya—of the subtle body
avinivrute—until reaching kaivalya
tasmat duhkham—life is therefore full of duhkha
svabhavena—happens naturally, can't be avoided

// The inherent nature of life is duhkha, suffering. All beings suffer from the fear of death. Everyone goes through old age and death, and that process creates duhkha until kaivalya is reached. An old man experiences more duhkha than a young man in this regard. Therefore, duhkha is unavoidable in this transmigration, however rich or powerful you may be. So all the riches, knowledge, and power you may possess are not going to help you overcome duhkha; the only way to overcome it is practice so as to not be born again. //

As the Yoga Sutras (2.15) say,

Parinama tapa samskara duhkhaih guna vrittih virodhat cha duhkham eva sarvam vivekinah

Things change over time and objects that were good and favorable once may become painful later on; this is called parinama duhkha. The inability to get what one wants and inability to get rid of what one does not want despite one's best efforts is called tapa duhkha, or pain of frustration. Since habits die hard, repeated states of pain and sorrow leave a

deep scar, and many do not get out of this dark hole; this is called samskara duhkha.

Even if you have a blessed life, ultimately duhkha catches up with you. Instead of going through this process lifetime after lifetime, why not employ the methods of Samkhya and Yoga? Because if you don't, when you get older this duhkha is not going away, so why not practice to remove it permanently and definitively, so you don't have to go through any number of rebirths. Before you reincarnate to again suffer old age and death, why not take another path? Just put time and effort in this direction, and you'll be on the path of eventual liberation that will set a higher spiritual course for you in case you are reborn.

Question: Is there any aspect of Samkhya that differs from Yoga?
Answer: Basically, the core of these two philosophies is the same. They both subscribe to the concept of the twenty-five tattvas. The Yoga Sutras (2.19) put it differently:

Visesa avisesa lingamatra alingani gunaparvani

Gross elements, subtle evolutes, the buddhi tattva, and mulaprakriti are the manifestations of the gunas.

Here the evolution described by Samkhyas is described in the reverse order to be in line with the yogi's progress toward kaivalya. *Visesha* refers to material objects made of the five gross elements. *Avisesha* refers to all the subtle aspects—the tanmatras, the eleven sense organs, and the self-identification or ego principle. *Lingamatra* refers to one aspect of prakriti, the intellect, or buddhi/mahat, which finally merges into the balanced state of the gunas known as *nirodha*, or cessation of desires and clinging. *Alinga* refers to the mulaprakriti, and at the individual level it would be the citta in a state of balance of the three gunas.

Samkhya and Yoga do not really differ in the sense that

Yoga helps us achieve the same goal as Samkhya, which is kaivalya. Not everyone has the capacity for Samkhya, so yogis came up with something to help anyone who is interested in eliminating duhkha. Lower-level aspirants still have distractions of the mind; they may be significantly rajasic or highly tamasic, but still interested in kaivalya. They too want duhkha to go away. For such people, the system of Yoga is effective, and there is a choice of three types, Kriya yoga, Ashtanga yoga, and Samadhi yoga.

Samkhya by itself alone may be sufficient for the more evolved person. Say a highly sattvic person almost from birth. Such a person can go into samadhi relatively easily, but for most people the depth of their understanding is only at the level of understanding by reading the authentic texts or scriptures (the *agama* level). They cannot progress to a state of better understanding through analysis and contemplation (the *anumana* level). They cannot go to the level of direct perception and realization (the *pratyaksha* level). For these people there has to be a different method, an accessible one. That method is Yoga.

So if you are a person with plenty of duhkha and unable to concentrate, start with Kriya yoga. Employ practices like controlling the tongue (speech and eating), because the tongue can be distracted by too much frivolous talk or make one a slave to food. And similarly proceed with the other senses.

Kārikā 56

Prakriti works for the ultimate release from samsara and moksha.

इत्येषप्रकृतिकृतोमहदादिविशेषभूतपर्यन्तः ।
प्रतिपुरुषविमोक्षार्थंस्वार्थैवपरार्थारम्भः ॥५६॥

Ityeṣaprakṛtikṛtomahadādiviśeṣabhūtaparyantaḥ |
pratipuruṣavimokṣārthaṃsvārthaivaparārthārambhaḥ ||56||

iti esah—in this way
prakriti krutah—due to the evolution of prakriti
mahadadi—from mahat to the last gross element
visesabhuta paryantah—till the individual elements
svartham iva—as though doing for itself
parartha—for the sake of the other
purusa pratiprurusa—for each and every individual purusha
vimoksartham—ultimate freedom, or kaivalya

// This universe is created not only to give us repeated births and deaths and to give duhkha in the process, but also so that prakriti can eventually give release to purusha. The same buddhi that has been leading us lifetime after lifetime evolves up to the point where there will be no more cittavrittis presented to the purusha, at which point we are completely released. The goal or capability of prakriti is thus to keep on giving experiences in bondage, lifetime after lifetime, in order to finally release purusha. //

It is said every creature during one human life or another will study Samkhya, Yoga, or Vedanta and make use of the prakritic body-mind complex to work toward ultimate release, or kaivalya/moksha. Prior to undertaking the spiritual path of Samkhya or Yoga, the ego, mind, and senses prevailed, but upon encountering dharma and experiencing disillusion with samsara, the buddhi then takes over. The Katha Upanishad tells us that we get attached to objects through the sense faculties (*indriyas*). When the influence of the senses is gradually weakened, the objects of the senses (*visayas*) overpower the senses. As paradoxical as this may sound, it is explained this way: What controls the senses is the mind, or the buddhi. Once the mind becomes stronger than the senses, the ego, or ahamkara, will recognize our attachment to the objects of the senses. This is when the buddhi takes over to facilitate the process of change and evolution, and to direct the ways and means of achieving total control over the senses. Thus prakriti works on behalf of purusha and the ultimate liberation of the person. As Patanjali's Yoga Sutras (2.18) confirm,

Prakasa kriya sthiti silam bhutendriyatmakam
bhogapavargartham drsyam

The entity seen as the individual person is made of the three gunas: sattva gives clarity and intelligence, rajas gives activity, and tamas gives inertia. It also consists of the five gross and five subtle elements and the thirteen sense organs. Its purpose is for giving varied worldly experiences and also for the release of the Self.

What we consider erroneously to be the Self (i.e., the physical self, or *drishya*) can incessantly give the experience of enjoyment (*bhoga*) or sensual pleasure to the person, but this, by and large, is only more duhkha. At some point the buddhi starts working in a different direction: toward final release or liberation. A yogi at some point in life decides to seek moksha. The mind realizes that this life cycle in samsara can't go on forever, so the person makes a concerted effort to achieve Patanjali's dictum of *citta vritti nirodha.*

When one feels the intense desire to become a yogi and stop the endless cycle of samsara, it is the buddhi, which is part of prakriti, that makes that decision. When we say, "I want to be released," we are referring to the purusha, even though the purusha is not part of the prakriti. The purusha, therefore, doesn't do anything; it is the prakriti, in the form of the buddhi, that takes us in this direction.

Kārikā 57

Just as nature provides milk for the nourishment of the calf, the same nature, or prakriti, works for moksha and the release of purusha.

वत्सविवृद्धिनिमित्तंक्षीरस्ययथाप्रवृत्तिरज्ञस्य ।
पुरुषविमोक्षनिमित्तंतथाप्रवृत्तिःप्रधानस्य ॥५७॥

Vatsavivṛddhinimittaṃkṣīrasyayathāpravṛttirajñasya |
puruṣavimokṣanimittaṃtathāpravṛttiḥpradhānasya ||57||

vasta vivrddhi nimittam—for the sake of nourishment of a baby calf
ajnasya ksirasy—milk that is insentient
pravrtte—is created, flows
yatha—in the way
ajnyasya—the one without consciousness, everything including the buddhi tattva, in the same way
pravrtte—functions
pradhanasya—an aspect of the creative principle, or mulaprakriti
purusa vimoksa nimittam—for the sake of the release of the purusha

// Just as the unintelligent flow of milk nourishes the baby calf, the prakriti does its job of giving bondage as well as leading us to freedom. The buddhi principle that is an aspect of prakriti is compared to milk—even though it does not have consciousness, milk does the work of nourishing the calf. So does the unconscious buddhi act to release purusha.

The ability to give duhkha due to ignorance, and also to give kaivalya, or freedom, are inherent capabilities of prakriti's buddhi principle. //

The purusha is not in bondage, but there is the feeling that it is still somehow trapped, which is a misconception that occurs because the buddhi does not understand the nature of purusha. And because it appears to be in bondage, we—that is, our thinking mind, our buddhi—wants to release it. As a result, the buddhi recognizes that it must take up the task of releasing the purusha. This may take one or many lifetimes, but gradually the buddhi takes control, and the ego self (*ahamkara*) falls in line. In due course it is able to understand the nature of purusha and attain its release.

Patanjali, in his Yoga Sutras (4.7), says,

Karma asukla akrishnam yoginah trividham itaresam

The karma of the yogi is neither white nor black; but the karma of the others is threefold.

For ordinary people, there are three types of karma: white, black, and mixed. Here white signifies dharma activities (or karma), black signifies adharmic activities (or karma), and mixed signifies activities that are a mixture of good and bad karma. But for the yogi, karma is neither white or black. Since the motive of the Raja yogi is to eschew worldly and otherworldly pleasures, the yogic karmas are neither white (or dharmic) nor black (or adharmic).

Most of us have a mixture of good and bad karma. Even the rituals we do are a mixture of good and bad activities. Most activities, dharmic or adharmic, lead to rebirth. If you do dharmic activities, you will progress higher; if you do adharmic activities, you'll go in the opposite direction. This is because both good deeds and bad deeds have motivation. But once the realization of the true nature of the Self dawns in the buddhi, there will be no motivation to do anything. That is why a yogi's karma is neither white nor black. Yogic activity does not add to the karma bundle, because in yoga there is no motivation to achieve in the outside world or the worlds beyond. You don't even want to go to heaven, let alone avoid going to the opposite place. You are not looking for anything for your own sake from the prakritic world. Samkhya and Yoga help you understand who you really are; they don't lead to the accumulation of karma, whether good or bad. As the Bhagavad Gita says in the chapter on Samkhya yoga,

Buddhi-yukto jahātīha ubhe sukṛita-duṣhkṛite
tasmād yogāya yujyasva yogaḥ karmasu kauśhalam

The wise one with a mind fully focused gives up both good and bad activities (*sukruta* and *dushkrita*). Yogic activities are neither good nor bad, and so do not create a karma bundle. So become a yogi. Of the three types, the good activities, the bad activities, and yogic activities, yogic activities are the most beneficial.

A wise person gives up both dharmic and adharmic karmas. What should one do then? Engage the mind in yoga. Why yoga? There are different types of karmas. There is pure (*sukla*) karma, in which good deeds lead to good experiences; bad or black (*krishna*) karma; and mixed (*sukla krishna*) karma. Then there is yogic karma, wherein you don't accumulate any karma at all. Yoga will not lead you to rebirth, so it is the best karma. However, if you die and have not yet reached the ultimate goal, according to Lord Krishna you will at least be reborn in a comfortable family or even in a yogi family to continue your yogic pursuits. So, yoga is a win-win system.

Kārikā 58

Just as people act to find happiness in the world, it is possible to get moksha with appropriate yogic efforts.

औत्सुक्यनिवृत्त्यर्थंयथाक्रियासुप्रवर्ततेलोकः ।
पुरुषस्यविमोक्षार्थंप्रवर्ततेतद्वदव्यक्तम् ॥५८॥

Autsukyanivṛttyarthaṃyathākriyāsupravartatelokaḥ |
puruṣasyavimokṣārthaṃpravartatetadvadavyaktam ||58||

yatha—in the same way
lokah—people, creatures in the world
outsukya—desires, happiness
vivrttyartham—fulfill
kriyasu pravartante—engage in various activities
tadvat—in the same way
avyakta—prakriti of the three gunas, especially the sattvic buddhi
purusasya vimoksartham pravartatnte—functions for the sake of the release of the purusha

// Just as ordinarily people strive with great intensity for worldly happiness, the buddhi of samkhyas and yogis acts with an equal intensity for the release or freedom of the purusha. In this way yogis and samkhyas are similar to those who pursue worldly goals, except that in the case of these aspirants their buddhi and their energy is not directed toward objects or desires. Some of us possess this focus and energy. Just as we focus on worldly activities, if we focus on spiritual activities, liberation is achievable. //

A strong man works with complete concentration to beat the other person. A warrior works with total concentration to defeat his enemy in war. A rich man focuses on making money, more and more and more. The person practicing dharma focuses on doing dharma and helping others. Just as we focus on worldly activities, if we focus on spiritual activities, moksha is achievable. And the chief spiritual activity is found in the philosophies of Samkhya and Yoga.

Kārikā 59

Like a dancer who leaves the stage after completing her performance, prakriti withdraws upon exhibiting purusha and providing the final act of kaivalya.

रङ्गस्यदर्शयित्वानिवर्ततेनर्तकीयथानृत्यात् ।
पुरुषस्यतथात्मानंप्रकाश्यविनिवर्ततेप्रकृतिः ॥५९॥

Raṅgasyadarśayitvānivartatenartakīyathānṛtyāt |
puruṣasyatathātmānaṃprakāśyavinivartateprakṛtiḥ ||59||

yatha—as
nartaki—a dancer
rangasya—of the theater
darsayitva—having exhibited her talents
nrtyat nivartate—withdraws from the dance
tatha—in the same way
prakrtih—prakriti in the form of the buddhi
purusasya—of the purusha
atmanam—its real nature

prakasya—having shown with clarity
nivartate—withdraws

// When the buddhi realizes that the purusha is not affected in any way by anything that the buddhi does, whether it is trying to earn more money or live hand to mouth, it will stop following this path and will withdraw from the world stage. The purusha remains unaffected. The poor man's purusha is not unhappy, nor is the rich man's purusha elated. //

There was a dancer in the king's court who performed regularly for the king. There was no communication between the king and the dancer. Every time she gave a good performance, she left the stage. She performed different dances for the king to keep him entertained. She grew into old age dancing for the king all her life. At a certain point she ran out of new varieties of dance to showcase for the king and started performing the same dance every time. One day an old man came to the court. She asked him, "I have been giving performances all these years. I keep changing my performance so that the king enjoys it. But I don't know whether he likes it or not." The old man said, "Don't you see, he is not at all interested in your dance. He watches because he has to watch. It does not matter whether your performance is good or not, or if you do or do not perform at all." So, the dancer stopped dancing, and the king missed nothing.

Now my buddhi is able to see that purusha does not require anything to make it happy. The buddhi, having known the true nature of the Self, will remain in the state of cessation of desires (*nirodha*) until the inevitable death comes. Death will not be painful or fearful for the realized yogi in a state of kaivalya.

Kārikā 60

Prakriti helps purusha reach freedom.

नानाविधैरुपायैरुपकारिण्यनुपकारिणःपुंसः ।
गुणवत्यगुणस्यसतस्तस्यार्थमपार्थकंचरति ॥६०॥

nānāvidhairupāyairupakāriṇyanupakāriṇaḥpuṃsaḥ |
guṇavatyaguṇasyasatastasyārthamapārthakaṃcarati ||60||

nana vidhaih upayaih—by several means (such as study, inference, asana, meditation, contemplation, and similar yogic pursuits)
upakarini—that which is helpful in reaching kaivalya, or the sattvic aspect
agunasya—to purusha, which has no prakritic characteristics (i.e., no sattva, rajas, or tamas)
satah—always
tasya—for that
pumsah—purusha
artha aparthakam carati—without a self-motive, prakriti acts

// The purusha does not have the twenty-four tattvas, but by some strange coincidence the purusha and prakriti tattvas are together. The buddhi is not able to see that. We consider the consciousness within us and the body as one composite unit and divide the universe into subject (the "I") and object (all the rest). We consider ourselves to be the subject, but in reality, we—that is, the prakritic body-mind complex—are part of the objective universe. //

Here Ishvarakrishna is comparing the roles of prakriti and purusha. All activities are done by prakriti—purusha does not do anything. But without purusha, no prakritic activity is possible. And without purusha, nothing will be experienced. All my experiences throughout my lifetime are because of prakriti providing these experiences and my purusha witnessing them.

When purusha gets very close to prakriti, evolution starts: mahat tattva, ahamkara tattva, buddhi tattva—all the rest of them come and appear to surround purusha. This happens to each and every person's purusha according to Samkhya. In the process of reaching kaivalya, purusha does nothing whatsoever. It just stays put. In this way prakriti functions for the sake of purusha. Both purusha and prakriti get nothing in the process. But if the buddhi does not see this, then duhkha occurs.

Kārikā 61

Once kaivalya is reached, prakriti never again bothers purusha.

प्रकृतेःसुकुमारतरं न किञ्चिदस्तीतिमेमतिर्भवति ।
यादृष्टास्मीतिपुनर्नदर्शनमुपैतिपुरुषस्य ॥६१॥

Prakṛteḥsukumāratarаṃnakiñcidastīti me matirbhavati |
yādṛṣṭāsmītipunarnadarśanamupaitipuruṣasya ||61||

prakrteh—of the prakriti
sukumarataram—ability to selflessly withdraw
na kincit asti—there is nothing like the way the prakriti functions
iti me matih—my view is that there is nothing like that

yaa drstah asmi—I have been seen or exposed
punah na darsanam upaiti—afterward it doesn't come in front of the purusha, it stays in a state of cessation

// The prakriti is constantly engaged in giving me experiences, lifetime after lifetime, mostly duhkha and sometimes happiness. Once kaivalya takes place, it withdraws completely. //

The knowledge of every aspect of prakriti is known and complete. After contemplating every aspect and stage of evolution and all twenty-five tattvas (including the purusha, the mulaprakriti of gunas, and the twenty-three prakritic evolutes), and once the buddhi understands and realizes the nature of prakriti, prakriti withdraws. This indicates that kaivalya is permanent, complete, and irreversible. Thereafter, prakriti doesn't provide any more experiences to purusha, because the mind has gone into *citta vritti nirodha*. Once kaivalya has taken place, there is no returning to the previous state.

Let's say you have reached kaivalya. The cittavrittis are no longer arising, and there is a certain tranquility. People come to you and say, "You are a great yogi, you are a realized yogi. We are going to hold a spiritual conference. We have gotten permission from the appropriate government agencies to flatten Mount Everest and create a huge area so that many thousands of people will come to this rarified spiritual place. Why don't you come too and be our honored guest and give a keynote address?" But you are not interested and will simply say, "No thanks." Because the buddhi has withdrawn, it is not interested in giving any kind of experience to purusha. Once the buddhi knows that purusha does not require anything to make it happy or unhappy, nothing can distract it. This is simple logic.

Kārikā 62

The real state of purusha

तस्मान् न बध्यतेऽद्धा न मुच्यतेनापिसंसरतिकश्चित् ।
संसरतिबध्यतेमुच्यते च नानाश्रयाप्रकृतिः ॥६२॥

Tasmānnabadhyate'ddhānamucyatenāpisaṃsaratikaścit |
saṃsaratibadhyatemucyate ca nānāśrayāprakṛtiḥ ||62||

tasmat—therefore
kascit—no one
na badhyate—is never in bondage (because it never undergoes any change)
napi mucyate—because it is not in bondage, there is no question of release
naapi kascit samsarati—nor does it transmigrate
prakrtih—the prakriti
nanasraya—in various roles
samsarati—moves around, transmigrates
badhyate—is in bondage
mucyate ca—and also released

// Prakriti ties itself in knots by thinking it is going to give experiences to purusha. It releases itself by understanding the nature of purusha. The mind is in bondage because of ignorance; once the realization comes that purusha does not require anything, then it is released. //

Here we note that all activities are done by prakriti only, and nothing but observation of the cittavrittis is the job of purusha. The buddhi, an important aspect of prakriti because of the tendency to remain ignorant of the true nature of purusha, mistakenly considers the body-mind complex as the Self. This is *avidya*, spiritual ignorance. But due to the study of Samkhya and the practice of Raja yoga in its entirety, the buddhi is eventually able to directly see or experience the nature of the Self. With that direct perception—what is known as *yougika pratyaksha*—the buddhi knows the truth, and with that, spiritual ignorance is eradicated and one attains absolute, irrevocable peace. That state is kaivalya, or freedom, which is the goal of Yoga and Samkhya. With that, all the three duhkhas are completely and permanently eradicated.

Kārikā 63

Kaivalya only comes about as a result of knowledge.

रूपैःसप्तभिरेवतुबध्नात्यात्मानमात्मनाप्रकृतिः ।
सैव च पुरुषार्थंप्रतिविमोचयत्येकरूपेण ॥६३॥

Rūpaiḥsaptabhirevatubadhnātyātmānamātmanāprakṛtiḥ |
saiva ca puruṣārthaṃprativimocayatyekarūpeṇa ||63||

prakrtih eva—prakriti alone
tu—certainly
purusartham—for the sake of purusharthas
prati—toward that
saptabhir upaih—in seven different forms (dharma, vairagya, aishwarya, adharma, ajnana, avairagya, and anaishwarya)
atmana atmanam badhnati—binds itself
ekarupena—by one form (jnana)
vimocayati—releases itself

// Out of the various sattvic and tamasic attitudes of the buddhi, seven of these will keep one in bondage. Some are worse than others. Even dharma is binding, therefore dharma is not a permanent solution. One must come to understand the true nature of the Self. Making the mind sattvic is the first requirement. //

In this sloka, Ishvarakrishna talks about the eight different directions the buddhi can take: righteousness (*dharma*), knowledge (*jnana*), detachment (*viraga*), and superior ability (*aisvarya)*, and their opposites—*adharma*, *ajnana*, *aviraga*, and *anaisvarya*. Out of these, only knowledge, jnana, brings about release; all the others keep you in bondage.

- A dharmic person will still be in bondage, but going to a higher place and experiencing more happiness.
- When you follow wickedness and immorality (*adharma*), you go to places where you experience intense unhappiness.
- When you are in ignorance (*ajnana*), you continue to consider the body to be the Self and do everything to satisfy this pseudo-self.
- When you develop detachment from worldly things (*viraga*), you dissolve the mind into its nature (*prakritilaya*) and you merge into one aspect of prakriti.
- When you have worldly attachments (*aviraga*), they will lead to more and more bondage.
- Mastery over prakriti (*aisvarya*) is found in the various siddhis, but keeps one still in bondage.

If you go after various aspects of prakriti and manage to attain mastery of the three sattvic methods (dharma or right conduct, dispassion, and siddhis), but you are still involved with any of the four tamasic activities (unwholesome activities, ignorance of the nature of the Self, attachment, and servitude), you will still be in bondage. Tamasic approaches will make you more and more unhappy. Sattvic approaches may make you less unhappy, but they still will not give permanent release. Only the sattvic mode of jnana—a thorough understanding of the nature of the Self and the twenty-four prakritic tattvas—will release you from the three types of duhkha permanently and definitively.

Kārikā 64

The importance of diligent practice and understanding the twenty-five tattvas

एवंतत्त्वाभ्यासान्नास्मि न मेनाहमित्यपरिशेषम् ।
अविपर्ययाद्विशुद्धंकेवलमुत्पद्यतेज्ञानम् ॥६४॥

Evaṃtattvābhyāsānnāsmina me nāhamityapariśeṣam |
aviparyayādviśuddhaṃkevalamutpadyatejñānam ||64||

evam—in this way
tattva abhyasat—contemplating the twenty-five tattvas
na asmi—what I think as the Self is not the Self (inferring the presence of *asmita*, or pride)
na me—this particular body belongs to the prakriti, is not of the purusha (inferring the presence of *mamata*, or selfishness)
na aham—I am the purusha, not the prakritic person seen
aparisesat—without any residue of doubt whatsoever
aviparyayat—no doubt about it, without the wrong notion that the prakritic body is the Self
visuddham—pure

kevalam—sure or kaivalya /freedom
utpadyate viveka jnanam—arises this distinctive knowledge

// Whatever I (my buddhi, my thinking faculty) have been thinking as the "I" is not the I anymore or ever was. This particular physical body belongs to prakriti, not to purusha. I am not this body, I am the Self, purusha. I am not this body, despite the feeling I have for this body (*asmita*), the feeling that I am this body. This body is not mine, it belongs to prakriti, not to purusha; I have no doubt about this. //

A clear understanding of purusha takes place without any doubt whatsoever when we completely understand the twenty-five tattvas, which are also discussed in the Yoga Sutras. This knowledge (*jnana*) leads to the aspirant's liberation. We need to study and contemplate the tattvas to acquire a correct understanding—study them over and over again with great concentration. We can improve our concentration by practicing yoga. Then the obstacle of thinking I am this body will be gradually eliminated. Knowledge of the tattvas will then arise in the mind of the practitioner.

Ishvarakrishna talks about practices for transcending the prakritic tattvas (*tattvabhyasa*) in order to achieve kaivalya, while Patanjali, in his Yoga Sutras, also talks about the importance of yogic practices (*abhyasa*) and the need to cultivate detachment in order to achieve his dictum of *citta vritti nirodha*. For Patanjali, abhyasa, or practice, means the practice of yoga. And what kind of yoga practice? Many people might think of asana practice, as many identify yoga as only being Hatha yoga's emphasis on physical postures. However, here we find that the practices recommended by Patanjali refer to yogic contemplation of the twenty-five tattvas, which leads one to determine what is not the Self in order to arrive at an understanding of the true nature of the Self. In this—that knowledge, jnana, is the key—the sage Panchashikha teaches us that Ishvarakrishna concurs:

पञ्च विंशति तत्वञः यत्र कुत्रश्रमे रतः।
जठी मुण्डी शिखी वापि मुच्यते नात्र संशयः॥

Pañca viṃśati tatvañaḥ yatra kutraśrame rataḥ |
jaṭhī muṇḍī śikhī vāpi mucyate nātra saṃśayaḥ ||

The one who thoroughly understands the twenty-five tattvas as shown by Samkhya will achieve final freedom irrespective of external appearances, like whether one grows matted hair, has a shaved head, or a long beard, or in whatever stages of life one may be in like a student, family person, retiree, or renunciate.

The aspirant who possesses knowledge of the twenty-five tattvas as articulated in Samkhya (the purusha; the mulaprakriti made up of the three gunas; the buddhi, or intelligence; the ahamkara, or the cosmic driving force or individual ego; the five tanmatras and the five gross elements; and the eleven indriyas) will attain everlasting freedom, moksha, and of that there is absolutely no doubt. It does not matter what stage of life you are in, whether you are a student, a householder, a retiree, or a renunciate. It does not matter if you wear robes, matted hair, are clean-shaven, or sport a tuft or a long beard. None of these external appearances, often used to impress others, really matter. What matters is knowledge of mulaprakriti, the twenty-three prakritic evolutes, and above all, a clear understanding of the nature of the witness or seer known as the Self, the purusha.

Here Ishvarakrishna uses a familiar term, *abhyasa* to indicate the kind of regular, concerted practice—the same term used by Lord Krishna in the Gita and by Patanjali in the Yoga Sutras, which in effect says, "Do it or lose it." The following is a story from ancient times that illustrates the importance of regular spiritual practice:

In the olden days, people used to propitiate the designated

nature gods. For example, to get abundant rain, farmers would make offerings to the rain god, Varuna, for copious rains. And the rain god, pleased with their offerings, would oblige the farmers with seasonal rains. The farmers would cultivate the land just before the rainy season, especially in the vast areas of India that depended on rainwater alone for cultivation, since there aren't any significant bodies of water in those regions. The farmers' livelihoods in those areas depended entirely on the mercy of the rain god, and so they did not want to get on the wrong side of Varuna. But then some young farmers, progressive farmers, reasoned that rain is a natural phenomenon and does not depend on the gods. This view slowly gained acceptance among the other farmers, who loathed the enormous rain ritual done every year. So one particular year the farmers decided to refrain from making offerings to Varuna.

Varuna, as the story goes, was extremely unhappy, furious even. He wanted to teach those farmers a lesson. But the rain god had a dharmic agreement with Lord Shiva. In that agreement it was stipulated that once Lord Shiva made a rumbling sound with his damaru, a handheld drum, Varuna must oblige by pouring rain down on the earth. So, Varuna approached the Lord to request that he refrain from using the drum for ten years to punish the insubordinate peasants. The Lord agreed, and there were no damaru rumblings, which resembled the rumbling of thunder before it rains, presumably for ten years.

The farmers were reeling under the ill effects of severe drought. Having found out that under Varuna's curse it might not rain for ten years, they even stopped cultivating their lands. But one farmer would nevertheless cultivate his fields every year before the rainy season, despite the drought. The other farmers, hungry as a result of not growing food, ridiculed the cultivating farmer for his futile efforts. When they asked him why he was cultivating the land even when he knew it likely wouldn't rain, the farmer said, "If I stop this activity for ten years, when the time comes to plant, I would have lost touch with the proper means of cultivation." The others just continued their ridicule of him.

Goddess Parvati, Shiva's feminine counterpart, was in the vicinity of the farmer's home at that time, gracing the local Shakti temple. When she overheard what had been going on, she immediately rushed to the blissful Shiva and asked him to play his damaru. Shiva was perplexed at this request and told her that he and Varuna had an agreement that he would not play his damaru for ten years. Parvati immediately told Shiva about the conversation she had overheard moments ago and told him that the lone farmer was cultivating the land even when he knew there would not be any rain for ten years, because he did not want to become rusty and not be able to do a satisfactory job of cultivating the land because of lack of practice, abhyasa. She told the Lord that if He refrained from using His dear drum for ten years, He would lose his facility with the drum. That got through to the Lord, who loved his drum and the gentle rumblings it would produce, so He took his damaru at once and played it with gusto. The rain god Varuna, who by nature's dharma was required to cause the rain to fall upon hearing the rumbling of the Lord's drum, gave copious rain, despite his earlier refusal to send rain down. And the farmer who had cultivated the land was ready to reap the benefits of copious rain. But the other farmers who had not cultivated the land and were out of practice lost out. They even lost the touch for plowing the land.

Patanjali, in the Yoga Sutras, describes practice, abhysas, as constantly putting forth effort and staying regular with one's practice. We must practice over a long period of time, with great focus. Why? Because we are trying to replace an old set of samskaras, or habits, with a new set of samskaras that involve a commitment to diligent practice. This kind of commitment applies to all profound activities, such as finding the method of ending the three forms of suffering and attaining eternal freedom.

Kārikā 65

The state of purusha and prakriti in kaivalya

तेननिवृत्तप्रसवामर्थवशात्सप्तरूपविनिवृत्ताम्
।प्रकृतिंपश्यतिपुरुषःप्रेक्षकवदवस्थितःसुस्थः॥६५॥

tenanivṛttaprasavāmarthavaśātsaptarūpavinivṛtt
prakṛtiṃpaśyatipuruṣaḥprekṣakavadavasthitaḥsuthaḥ ||65||

tena—by this, thereby
nivritta prasavam—ceases to produce; the citta, which has incessantly been presenting experience after experience to the purusha, now doesn't create any new experiences
pursharthavasat—having understood the nature of the purusha
saptarupavinivrttam—having refrained from the seven types of *vrittis*, or thoughts (*dharma/adharma, ajnana, viraga/aviraga, aisvarya/anaisvarya*)
svacchah—remaining in itself without any association with prakriti
avasthitah—without any activity
preksavat—like a spectator in a theater
purushah—purusha, the Self
arthavasath—having reached the goal of kaivalya
prakritim—the prakriti
pasyati—witnesses

// **The purusha sees the whole process. It is able to see without participating in the whole thing, can simply witness the arising**

cittavrittis. The purusha has been witnessing a lot of turmoil in the prakritic mind; the buddhi ultimately understands the nature of the Self and consequently the cessation of all activities of the citta ensues (*citta vritti nirodha*). And the purusha is able to see the citta in the state of *nirodha*, or cessation. The prakriti remains in its true state of equilibrium, while the purusha is simply a spectator. //

The purusha is able to experience the aspirant's process of going from the state of a multitude of cittavritis arising, to a state of *citta vritti nirodha*, or cessation of the ceaselessly arising cittavrittis, and is thus ultimately able to see these resolving back into the equilibrium of the three gunas. This is called *samyavastha* in yoga, referring to a state of balance or equilibrium of the gunas. This says that the purusha that experiences everything that goes on in the citta as vrittis—good, bad, or indifferent—will also witness the process of *citta vritti nirodha*.

Kārikā 66

A complete understanding and withdrawal of the buddhi

दृष्टामयेत्युपेक्षकैकोदृष्टाहमित्युपरतान्या ।
सतिसंयोगेऽपितयोःप्रयोजनंनास्तिसर्गस्य ॥६६॥

Dṛṣṭāmayetyupekṣakaikodṛṣṭāhamityuparatānyā |
sati saṃyoge'pitayoḥprayojanaṃnāstisargasya ||66||

maya iti upekshka—he is not affected at all
Ekah—refers to the purusha, that which remains as witness remains in the theater

drstaha—the prakriti has been seen or exposed
iti—thus
upekshakah—remains disinterested
anyaa—the other, the prakriti
aham drashta—I am exposed (as the purusha has seen all twenty-four aspects of prakriti)
iti—thus
uparamati—withdraws
atah—therefore
tayoh—between the two, prakriti and purusha
samyoge sati—as long as there is association (i.e., until death)
sargasya—during the remainder of life
prayojanam—use or achievement
nasti—is nil

// The purusha does not require anything, so for the buddhi, with this understanding, there is no reason or motivation to take another birth. Even though samskaras may still remain, because the veil of ignorance (*avidya*) has been removed, there will be no impetus to take another birth. //

Once I (that is, my buddhi, my intellect) have realized the real nature of the Self directly, through yogic perception, there will be no further activity of the mind, or cittavrittis. I will not be disturbed at all by the external world, and there will be no question of taking another birth.

The Yoga Sutras (2.13) say this in no uncertain terms:

Sathimule tadvipako jaatiayurbogaha

As long as *avidya*, or ignorance of the Self, is not eradicated or uprooted, the unripened karmas in the karma bundle will ripen, leading to a new birth in a particular species, with a span of life and life experiences.

These are the two things that will cause another birth: ignorance, *avidya*, and unripened karma.

Kārikā 67

With knowledge of the tattvas, purusha, as witness, watches prakriti, which has ceased to be productive and has turned back from the seven vrittis that keep one in bondage.

सम्यग्ज्ञानाधिगमाद्धर्मादीनामकारणप्राप्तौ
तिष्ठतिसंस्कारवशाच्चक्रभ्रमवद्धृतशरीरः ॥६७॥

Samyagjñānādhigamāddharmādīnāmakāraṇaprāptau |
tiṣṭhatisaṃskāravaśāccakrabhramavaddhṛtaśarīraḥ ||67||

samyak—thorough

jnana—understanding of the twenty-five tattvas (not just via bookish knowledge, but by deep contemplation and yogic samadhi)

adigamath—direct perception

dharmadinam—the seven other approaches (dharma, etc.)

akaarana praptau—they are not capable of doing anything because they are the ones that will lead one to rebirth.

tishtathi—remains (as long as we are held in the body)

samskaravasat—some samskaras remain, like breathing, feeling hungry, etc.

chakra—the potter's wheel

brahmavath—keeps on rotating for a few more rounds
dritha—remains until death, prana will do its function

When ignorance (*avidya*) is gone, rebirth will not take place, even though one may have old karma remaining. One will not be propelled into another birth, as one is able to understand the nature of the purusha and remain in cessation (*nirodha*) for the duration of the life. A nirodha citta cannot transmigrate.

There are two types of cittavrittis. One is the cittavritti that Patanjali talks about: the cittavrittis that are unique to each individual. As well, the Samkhya Karika describes the other type of vritties, or activities of the mind: the *samanyakarana vrittis*, the general activity that maintains life through the breath, or prana. That will continue regardless of one's realization of the nature of the Self. *Citta vritti nirodha* has already taken place, but the *samanyakarana vrittis*, the general activities of the citta, or brain, that maintain life, will continue for the duration of the lifetime.

How does a yoga practitioner become a consummate yogi? When a thorough understanding of the twenty-five tattvas occurs as a direct perception, not merely as a result of bookish knowledge or inference, but as a complete conviction. The seven approaches—*dharma/adharma*, *ajnana*, *viraga/aviraga*, *ishvarya/anaishvarya*—can not bring this about because these approaches will lead to rebirth, whether good, bad, or indifferent. With these seven approaches there are still some samskaras remaining. Then there are the innate samskaras that sustain life and keep one breathing, feeling hungry, and so forth, the *samanyakarana vrittis*. After the potter completes the work of crafting a pot, the potter's wheel keeps on rotating for a few more rounds. Similarly, as long as one is holding a body and until death, prana, the life force, will continue. To outsiders, the realized yogi will appear to be just be like other people, except that what goes on in his or her mind is different from what goes on in others' minds. Nothing actually is going on in their mind—there are no attachments, and there is an absolute sense of peace. He or she may be completely oblivious to the outside world and rarely be aware of their own body, spending most of their time in nirodha samadhi, and only occasionally emerging from this state. In *samyavastha*, the state of yogic equilibrium, the mind is absolutely peaceful, as there is nothing to do and nothing to know. The yogi will remain in that state until death takes place naturally.

Here is a story about Shukha, the son of the sage Vyasa and the main narrator of the Bhagavata Purana. Shukha was a *jivan mukta*, a self-realized yogi, the Vedanta equivalent of the state of Samkhya kaivalya. One day he was walking and passed by a pond where a number of women were bathing. They never bothered to cover themselves as Shukha passed by. A few moments later, Shukha's father, the great sage Vyasa, came along the same way. Seeing Vyasa, the women hurried to cover themselves. Vyasa stopped and asked them how come they never bothered to cover themselves upon seeing his son but acted differently when he, a much older person, came along. The women said that Shukha was completely oblivious to the outside world. They told him that Shukha was in *nirvikalpa samadhi*, a meditative state of total absorption and bliss, all the time, barely aware of his own physical person. But you, they said, are like other people, and we do what we do when ordinary people pass by.

Kārikā 68

Permanent cessation of duhkha

प्राप्तेशरीरभेदेचरितार्थत्वात्प्रधानविनिवृत्तौ ।
ऐकान्तिकमात्यन्तिकमुभयंकैवल्यमाप्नोति ॥६८॥

Prāpteśarīrabhedecaritārthatvātpradhānavinivṛttau |
aikāntikamātyantikamubhayaṃkaivalyamāpnoti ||68||

iekanthikam atyantikam ubhayam—ending of dhukha is both permanent and definitive
sharirabedheprapthe—when separation from the body takes place at the time of death
charirtharthatvat—the object is to know the real nature of the Self
pradhana vinivrthou—when the prakriti ceases to act, the path of turning inward will bring cessation
kaivalyam apnoti—attains kaivalya or freedom, but until the time of death one will still be associated with the body

// Many known efforts for getting beyond duhkha are neither permanent nor definitive. But the ending of duhkha is both permanent and definitive when one has attained the true knowledge of the purusha. When that happens and the separation from the body takes place at the time of death, the goal has been achieved. What is the goal? It is to know the true nature of the Self—that kaivalya has been achieved when the prakriti ceases to act. Such a person will not be born again to suffer the effects of three causes of pain. //

This sloka is describing what happens when one achieves the goal of the cessation of duhkha. Once this takes place, one does not worry about a "relapse." There will be no such relapse. This is definite—there is no other method. Kaivalya, or moksha, is the total release at the time of death. Why does Ishvarakrishna say total kaivalya toward the end? Because until the time of death, one is still associated with the body. So samkhyas say that at the time of death, once kaivalya has been realized, there is absolutely no reason to believe that one will take another birth.

Kārikā 69

Goal of the Samkhya Karika achieved

पुरुषार्थज्ञानमिदंगुह्यंपरमर्षिणासमाख्यातम् ।
स्थित्युत्पत्तिप्रलयाश्चिन्त्यन्तेयत्रभूतानाम् ॥६९॥

Puruṣārthajñānamidaṃguhyaṃparamarṣiṇāsamākhyātam |
sthityutpattipralayāścintyante yatra bhūtānām ||69||

idam—this
guhyam—spiritual knowledge that is not commonly known, or is obscure, something hidden
purusharta jnanam—the goal of knowledge about the purusha
paramarsinam—given by great rishis
samakhyatam—explained completely and thoroughly
bhutanam—creatures
sthiti utpatti pralaya—sustenance, the creation and then dissolution
purushartha jnanam—able to understand the purusha (then everything about prakriti in its stage of creation, sustenance and finally dissolution)

// In this text, what is known? It talks about creatures, it talks about sustenance (*sthiti*), it talks about the creation (*utpatthi*), then it talks about the final dissolution (*pralaya*). If you are able to

understand the purusha, then everything about the prakriti in its stages of creation, sustenance, and dissolution is understood. //

This spiritual knowledge is not commonly known; it is obscure. It is something hidden—you don't know it is there. We go around and around, not knowing what is available to us. Knowledge about the purusha is not available everywhere. It is given by great rishis, accomplished masters who speak the truth. Such a truth-teller speaks nothing other than the truth—that is why they are called rishis.

Kārikā 70

The secret knowledge concerning the liberation of the purusha given by a succession of masters

एतत्पवित्रमग्र्यंमुनिरासुरयेऽनुकम्पयाप्रददौ ।
आसुरिरपिपञ्चशिखायतेनबहुधाकृतंतन्त्रम् ॥७०॥

Etatpavitramagryaṃmunirāsuraye'nukampayāpradadau |
āsurirapipañcaśikhāyatenabahudhākṛtaṃtantram ||70||

etat—this
pavitram—very pure
agryam—very high, in front of, forerunner
munih, agrahmunih—the forerunner is the sage Kapila
asuraye—taught to his follower Asuri
anukampaya—he taught due to his compassion for people suffering
panchashikha—from Asuri to the sage Panchashikha

bahuda—other people
kratam tantram—this philosophy was handed down by a succession of teachers
ishvarakrishna—ultimately including Ishvarakrishna

// This very pure, very highly respected subject was taught by Kapila the sage to his chief disciple, Asuri, due to Kapila's compassion; then transmitted by Asuri to Panchashikha; then by him to other people, who have been taught by a succession of teachers that ultimately include Ishvarakrishna, the author of this text. This is the lineage of these teachings (*sishya parampara*). //

This is not something Ishvarakrishna wrote while sitting under a banyan tree, contemplating his navel. This is traditional knowledge handed down by a succession of teachers and masters.

Kārikā 71

Gratitude

शिष्यपरम्परयागतमीश्वरकृष्णेनचैतदार्याभिः ।
सङ्क्षिप्तमार्यमतिनासम्यग्विज्ञायसिद्धान्तम् ॥७१॥

Siṣyaparamparayāgatamīśvarakṛṣṇenacaitadāryābhiḥ |
saṅkṣiptamāryamatināsamyagvijñāyasiddhāntam ||71||

sisya paramparaya—a succession of teachers, a lineage
agatam—having come
isvara krsnena—by Ishvarakrishna

aryabhih—in the arya meter
samyak vijnaya—having thoroughly understood
siddhantha—this particular philosophy
samkshiptam—in a concise manner
aryamatinah—by the great intellectual

// Following in a succession of teachers, this lineage culminates with the noble Ishvarakrishna. After studying the subject of Samkhya thoroughly and having spent time understanding this philosophy, Ishvarakrishna wrote this brief work in the beautiful arya meter. //

Kārikā 72

Concluding Remarks

सप्तत्यांकिलयेऽर्थास्तेऽर्थाःकृत्स्नस्यसृष्टितन्त्रस्य ।
आख्यायिकाविरहिताःपरवादविवर्जिताश्चाऽपि॥७२॥

Saptatyāṃkilaye'rthāste'rthāḥkṛtsnasyasṛṣṭitantrasya |
ākhyāyikāvirahitāḥparavādavivarjitāścā'pi ||72||

shashtitantrasya—of the text called Shastitanrea
kritsnasya—which is a comprehensive shastra
ye arthah—those topics
te—they
akhyayikavirahita—without stories
paravadavivarjitas ca—without being involved in debating other philosophies
saptatyat—in seventy verses

// The subject that is treated in this seventy-verse work follows a text called the Shasti Tantra, which was prevalent in ancient times. The Shasti Tantra contains the main doctrine found in the karikas, and I have written this text without any illustrative stories. Other texts deal with the other philosophies. This is written mainly to explain what this philosophy is, rather than trying to find fault or contradict other philosophies. //

And that is the end of the text.

What next? Probably the writer will write another book, the editor will edit another book, the publisher will surely publish another book, and the habitual book reader will read another book.

But what did the reader get out of reading the Samkhya philosophy, especially the Ishvarakrishna presentation? It is the most important message of the truth about what constitutes the true Self—what should be called "I." It is not the mind-body complex, but the unvarying immortal consciousness. This thesis is echoed by the two nivritti philosophies, Yoga and Vedanta, as explicated in the Vedas and Upanishads and Yoga Sutras. By defining the Self as the *jnah*, the knower or experiencer, Ishvarakrishna defines the Self as neither a product nor a producer, implying that the Self has no beginning or end, and hence is immortal. That the true Self is immortal could, of course, be a challenging idea for many ordinary people to accept. After all, if I am immortal, why worry about death or any of the pain and sorrow inherent in life?

Lord Krishna in the Gita spends the first chapter, called "Samkhya Yoga," teaching Arjuna about the true nature of the Self, thereby drawing Arjuna out of the deep despair he was in. Patanjali in his Yoga Sutras underscores the importance of self-knowledge (*atma jnana*) in overcoming the pain and sorrow of life. Vedanta, in the Upanishads, talks about the nature of the Self as pure consciousness. The Vedas also contain many references to the immortality of the Self. The chapter in the Yajur Veda known as Aruna contains the pithy mantra *amrutam purushah*, meaning that the purusha, or indwelling consciousness, is immortal.

Among billions of people who have ever lived and will ever live on Earth, past, present, and future, who have had or will have the impression that the prakritic body-mind complex is the Self, perhaps only one person in a million may stumble into the study of Samkhya. Such rare individuals will receive the knowledge that the Self is immortal. Those of you who have read this book are among those who know this truth about the Self. Even though it is valid, this knowledge is only the first step—called *shruta prangna*, or secondhand information heard from a well-meaning scholar. Many people, curious but still unconvinced, go about reading more and more and continue to listen to scholars, but they still remain unsure. According to the old schools, the knowledge arising from reading books or listening to teachers is only the first step in knowing the truth. In worldly matters, one can understand the truth by direct perception if possible, but directly knowing the nature of the Self is not possible, as the senses, or *indriyas*, cannot really directly "see" the Self.

So, the second step of knowing the truth is to make use of your God-given intelligence to understand it by inference. The Upanishads, the Gita, and the Yoga Sutras all give some clues for the aspiring seeker to contemplate. The Gita says that the same Self that is aware of the various activities of the mind during childhood is the same Self that experiences different mental activities and thoughts during adulthood, and experiences the sobering thoughts and emotions that arise in old age, near the end of life—and even beyond, it is the same Self that experiences the next birth.

Patanjali infers the existence of purusha by pointing out that the ever-changing mental activities or cittavrittis are known only due to the existance of the unchanging purusha or consciousness (*sada jnathah cittavruttayah tat prabhoho purushasya aparinamatvat*). In the seventeenth sloka, the Samkhya Karika uses a metaphor to indicate the separate nature of the purusha by saying that a bed made of several parts is for the use of the person who sleeps there, not for the bed itself. Likewise, the body-mind assemblage is for the experience of the true Self, the purusha. The five-sheath example given in the Taitiriya Upanishad, which is quite popular among yoga students, talks about the human body being made of five sheaths of organic matter: prana, or the life force; the indriyas, the senses; the intellect, or buddhi or jnana; and finally the emotional sheath. The entity that exists beyond all these prakritic sheaths is the purusha, the true Self.

Patanjali's use of *cit* (consciousness) and *citta* (referring to the the brain's activities) is a masterstroke in terms of understanding the nature of the Self. As Lord Krishna points out in the Samkhya Yoga chapter in the Gita, all our experience of outside objects are only sensations. It is obvious that we do not see objects as such, but only receive the stimulation of the senses by the sense objects. Light particles, or rupa tanmatras, stimulate the eyes. The same is true for the other senses. These sensations reach the brain through their respective pathways such as the optic nerves or the auditory or olfactory nerves. All these sensations, according to Yoga and Samkhya, are first collated by the mind or manas, colored by ego or ahamkara, and analyzed by intellect or buddhi, which then make a projection called a cittavritti, which is presented to the purusha. The presentation also includes a picture of one's body. We are aware of our own body all the time except when we're asleep or in samadhi (or in a coma), when sensations are ignored by the brain. And the brain evolved out of organic matter, is sustained by organic matter, and finally disappears into the natural elements and has no consciousness. Then who experiences the various happenings in the brain as thoughts or cittavrittis? Samkhyas, yogis, and vedantins aver that it is the unchanging consciousness, which is variously called the atman, the purusha, jnah, or cit. The aspirant who wants to know the Self deduces the nature and existence of the Self by studying the nivritti philosophies, all of which lead to this conclusion. Each person should sit down and contemplate until the conviction that the unchanging consciousness is the true Self. Samkhyas call this process anumana, "inference," a process recognized by all Vedic philosophies.

But then as we have seen earlier, jnana, or knowledge of the Self, will accrue only in a sattvic mind or buddhi. Most minds are highly rajasic. So even though according to samkhyas the the upper regions (heavens) are permeated by sattva, the middle region—the world we live in—is highly rajasic, while the netherworlds are dominated by tamas. So most human beings who desire knowledge of the true Self and who overcome the three sources of suffering may at best only be able to *infer* the existence and nature of the Self. This is why even though there are many earnest aspirants, those who are able to directly experience the nature of the Self are few and far between. So many people who spend their lifetimes studying the nature of the Self keep reading, contemplating, and of course hoping for the spiritual jackpot.

We've seen in the Samkhya Karika that only a sattvic buddhi or intellect is capable of attaining knowledge of the atman. Among those with a sattvic temperament, many resort to dharma, or righteousness, to become compassionate and moral leaders. Some develop siddhi powers. Others become renunciates due to vairagya.

All of this is to show that the goal of kaivalya, the state in which one is able to transcend the three duhkhas, is very difficult and rare. However, even with secondhand knowledge and inferential conviction it would be helpful to go through life as a karma yogi, one devoted to selfless service, as in the case of Arjuna. But achieving kaivalya—the goal of Samkhya and Yoga—becomes possible only with further effort and refinements. That is where Yoga philosophy steps in. Since Yoga and Samkhya have the same philosophical base, one may wonder why a newer system such as Yoga is needed. Yoga makes it possible for everyone, even a rajasic person, to achieve kaivalya. Patanjali in his Yoga Sutras points out that the state of the mind of the yogi who has attained direct knowledge through yogic samadhi is qualitatively very different from the other two levels of understanding—secondhand information from teachers or books, and the conviction that comes out of inference. Here is the quote (Yoga Sutra 1.48):

ऋतम्भरा तत्र प्रज्ञा ॥ १.४८॥

ṛtambharā tatra prajñā

The yogic realization of the Self is full of truth, without an iota of doubt.

To use an expression popular in Tamil, my mother tongue, "It is as clear as a mountain in wide-open space" (*vellidai malai*). Another verse (Yoga Sutra 1.49) states,

श्रुतानुमानप्रज्ञाभ्यामन्यविषया विशेषार्थत्वात् ॥ १.४९॥

śrutānumānaprajñābhyāmanyaviṣayā viśeṣārthatvāt

It is a unique understanding/experience, entirely different from the understanding from hearing from experts or conviction arising out of deep contemplation and inference.

When you are convinced about the truth of the Self as enunciated by samkhyas, and you find that book knowledge and conviction alone are not sufficient, you have to make yourself fit for direct perception of the Self. Yoga as a first step can turn a predominantly tamasic or rajasic person into a sattvic person, which is the sine qua non for jnana and kaivalya. Patanjali recommends Kriya yoga for the rank beginner and Ashtanga yoga for one totally committed to eradicating duhkha forever. A practitioner of Ashtanga yoga's asana and pranayama who meticulously observes the first two steps of yama and niyama (a yogi's dos and don'ts) would have the mental space to eliminate tamas and rajas and become sattvic. The discipline of yoga is well-designed and tested. It helps the yoga practitioner reduce the dominance of tamas and rajas so that sattva can come up. A sattvic mind makes this practitioner fit for the samkhya's jnana, or knowledge of the Self. The predominantly rajasic mind—the state of most people—has a short attention span and a quick-moving train of thoughts, and of course both are impediments to reaching kaivalya.

The mind of a yogi in a state of samadhi is capable of seeing the nature of the Self directly. This state is called *yougika pratyaksha*, direct perception. One can trust the truth behind both the Samkhya and Yoga philosophies. The ancient sages associated with these systems are the rishis. A rishi is defined as one who speaks the truth and nothing but the truth (*rshayah satyavacasah*).

I wrote this book on the Samkhya Karika mainly for the benefit of yoga practitioners, looking at Samkhya as well as its sister philosophy, Yoga. May it bring benefit to all who read it!

GLOSSARY

abhinivesha: clinging to life out of fear of death
abhyasa: regular, committed spiritual practice
acharya: one who shows the path
adhi: pain
adhibhautika: suffering caused by other beings, one of the three causes of suffering
adhidaivika: suffering caused by nature, literally acts of god
adhyatmika: suffering caused by internal factors
adhyayana: study, study of scriptures
ahamkara: the cosmic driving force, self-identification or the individual ego principle, motivator to act; one of the twenty-five tattvas
ahimsa: do no harm
aisvarya: sovereignty, superior power over nature
akasha: space
anaisvarya: basically servitude (see aisvarya)
andhatamisra: deep darkness, fear of annihilation
antahkarana: three aspects of the mind—buddhi, manas, ahamkara
apara vairagya: lower state of detachment
apavarga: final release, process of attaining final release
asakti: incapacity
asat: nonexistence; the opposite of sat, Brahman
asmita: pride, the feeling that I am this body
asura: demon
atmajnana: knowledge of the Self
atman: the Self, purusha
avairagya: attachment; the opposite of vairagya/detachment
avidya: wrong knowledge, ignorance

aviraga: attachment
avisesha: nonspecific, absence of distinction, subtle
avisuddhi: impure
avyakta: the unmanifest source of the universe
bhava: experiences, feelings
bhoga: enjoyment, sensual pleasure, indulgence
bhutas: elements
buddhi: intellect, cosmic intelligence at the individual level; one of the twenty-five tattvas; see also mahat
capalya: craving
cit: consciousness
citta: brain
cittavrittis: thoughts, activities of the brain
dana: offering, donation
dharana: to hold, first stage of meditation in ashtanga yoga
divyam srotram: divine sounds
drashta: the seer, the witness, purusha (in Samkhya) or the Self; term used in Yoga philosophy
duhkha: suffering, vitiated mental space
duhkhavighatah: suppression of the three forms of suffering
dvesha: hatred, aversion
gunas: referring to the three qualities of sattva, rajas, and tamas
gunavaitrsnyam: highest form of dispassion
indriyas: sense organs
jivan mukta: a self-realized yogi; literally, one who attained liberation even while living
jnah: the knower, consciousness, awareness
jnana: knowledge
jnanendriyas: the organs of perception; the five sense organs (eyes, ears, nose, tongue, skin); one of the twenty-five tattvas
kaivalya: liberation, moksha; literally, to be alone, undisturbed, free
karanas: the organs of causation
karmendriyas: organs of action; the five motor organs (mouth, feet, hands, genitals, anus); one of the twenty-five tattvas
klesha: that which causes pain, obscurations

linga sarira: the subtle body

mahamoha: great delusion

mahat: literally the greatest; cosmic intelligence, individual intellect; one of the twenty-five tattvas

mahattattva: cosmic intelligence and universal order

mamata: selfishness

manas: mind that coordinates all the instruments of action and the senses, like eye-hand coordination, etc.; one of the twenty-five tattvas

moha: delusion

moksha: liberation (see kaivalya)

mulaprakriti: the root source of the universe possessing the three gunas in perfect equilibrium; one of the twenty-five tattvas

nidra: the sleeping state

nirodha: cessation of activity

nirvikalpa samadhi: a meditative state of absorption in the ultimate truth

nivritti: release from pain

pancha bhutas: the five gross elements of earth, water, fire, air, space; aspects of the twenty-four prakritic tattvas

pancha kleasas: five afflictions of the mind

para vairagya: higher level of detachment

parinama: change

pradhana: the source principle of nature (see mulaprakriti)

prakasa: to illuminate

prakriti: everything that is of the world of form; nature; the manifest universe

prakritilaya: one who is submerged in prakriti

pralaya: final dissolution

pramana: proof, correct knowing

pratyaya: tendencies, contents of the mind, one's mental mode

punya: virtue, merit

purusha: the Self; literally, the indwelling principle; pure, unvarying, immortal consciousness; the subject; one of the twenty-five tattvas

raga: an affliction, intense attachment
rupa: form
sabda: oral instruction, hearing
samanyakarana vritti: activities of the mind that are unconscious and autonomic, such as breathing
samkhya: a practitioner of Samkhya philosophy
samskara: deeply rooted habits, either beneficial or unfavorable for liberation
samyavastha: the state of yogic equilibrium of the three gunas
sat: eternal, real, pure, the absolute truth, existence
siddhi: accomplishment
smriti: recollection or remembering
sparsa: touching, feeling, contact with an object
sukshma sarira: subtle body
tamisra: feeling of failure to get what one wants
tanmatras: rudimentary subtle elements from which gross elements are formed (light, sound, taste, smell, touch); aspects of the twenty-five tattvas
tapa: heat, yearning
tattvas: principles or elements of reality
tushti: contentment, satisfaction, complacency
uhah: reasoning
vairagya: detachment, dispassion
vasikara: control
vedantin: a practitioner of Vedanta
videha: state in which one's awareness is not confined to the body, out of body existence of a yogi
vikalpa: fantasy, imagination
vikriti: "after creation," evolute, products
viparyaya: incorrect knowing
viraga: detachment
visaya: objects of the senses, objects of enjoyment, objects of knowledge
vrittis: activities, especially thoughts that surface in the mind
vyakta: the manifest universe

INDEX